A CENTURY OF POLITICAL CARTOONS

Caricature in the United States from 1800 to 1900

BY
ALLAN NEVINS
AND
FRANK WEITENKAMPF

WITH 100 REPRODUCTIONS OF CARTOONS

OCTAGON BOOKS

A DIVISION OF FARRAR, STRAUS AND GIROUX

New York   1975

Copyright 1944 by Charles Scribner's Sons
Copyright renewed © 1972 by Mary R. Nevins and Louise Suhl Weitenkampf

Reprinted 1975
by special arrangement with Charles Scribner's Sons

OCTAGON BOOKS
A Division of Farrar, Straus & Giroux, Inc.
19 Union Square West
New York, N. Y. 10003

Library of Congress Cataloging in Publication Data

Nevins, Allan, 1890-1971.
    A century of political cartoons.

  Reprint of the ed. published by Scribner, New York.

    1. United States—Politics and government—19th century—Caricatures and cartoons. 2. American wit and humor, Pictorial. I. Weitenkampf, Frank, 1866-1962, joint author. II. Title.

E337.5.N48   1975   973′.002′07   74-34276
ISBN 0-374-96092-5

Printed in USA by
Thomson-Shore, Inc.
Dexter, Michigan

CONTENTS

[1800] PROVIDENTIAL DETECTION	20
Etching. Library Company of Philadelphia. Ridgway Library	
[1801] MAD TOM IN A RAGE	22
Etching.	
[1799] SEE PORCUPINE, IN COLOURS JUST PORTRAY'D	22
Etching. Historical Society of Pennsylvania	
[1808] THE CAT LET OUT OF THE BAG	24
By William Charles. *Etching.* New York Public Library	
[1814] JOHN BULL MAKING A NEW BATCH OF SHIPS TO SEND TO THE LAKES	26
By William Charles. *Etching.*	
[1815] JOHNNY BULL AND THE ALEXANDRIANS	28
By William Charles. *Etching.* New York Public Library	
[1815] JOHN BULL BEFORE NEW ORLEANS	28
By William Charles. *Etching.* New York Public Library	
[1815] THE HARTFORD CONVENTION OR LEAP NO LEAP	30
By William Charles. *Etching.*	
[1824] A FOOT-RACE	32
By D. C. Johnston. *Etching.* New York Public Library	
[1829] A NEW MAP OF THE UNITED STATES, WITH THE ADDITIONAL TERRITORIES ON AN IMPROVED PLAN	34
Lithograph. Printed by Imbert. New York Public Library	
[1828] THE PEDLAR AND HIS PACK OR THE DESPERATE EFFORT, AN OVER BALANCE	36
Etching. New York Public Library	
[1831] A POLITICAL GAME OF BRAG. OR THE BEST HAND OUT OF FOUR	36
Lithograph. Published by H. R. Robinson. Printed by Pendleton, New York. American Antiquarian Society	
[1833] DESPOTISM—ANARCHY—DISUNION	38
Lithograph. Printed by Endicott & Swett. New York Public Library	
[1833] THE DOWNFALL OF MOTHER BANK	40
By "Zek Downing." *Lithograph. Published by H. R. Robinson.* American Antiquarian Society	
[1834] THE CELESTE-AL CABINET	40
Lithograph. Published by H. R. Robinson.	
[1834] OFFICE HUNTERS FOR THE YEAR 1834	42
Lithograph. Printed by Imbert. W. B. Osgood Field	
[1834] SYMPTOMS OF A LOCKED JAW	44
By D. C. Johnston. *Lithograph.* American Antiquarian Society	
[1836] THE DEBILITATED SITUATION OF A MONARCHAL [Sic!] GOVERNMENT	46
Lithograph.	

[1837] NEW EDITION OF MACBETH. BANK-OH'S GHOST 48
    By E. W. Clay. *Lithograph. Published by H. R. Robinson.*

[1837] THE MODERN BALAAM AND HIS ASS 50
    Lithograph.   *New York Public Library*

[1840] THE TIMES 52
    By E. W. Clay. *Lithograph. Published by H. R. Robinson.*

[1840] CLAR DE KITCHEN 54
    By Boneyshanks. *Lithograph. Published by H. R. Robinson.*
                                    American Antiquarian Society

[1844] POLITICAL CLIMBING BOYS 56
    Lithograph.   *New York Public Library*

[1844] ALL THE MORALITY AND ALL THE RELIGION 58
    Lithograph.   *New York Public Library*

[1846] FUNERAL OBSEQUIES OF FREE-TRADE 60
    By E. W. Clay. *Lithograph. Published by H. R. Robinson.*

[1846] THE GOOD BOY WHO GAVE AWAY HIS CAKE 60
    Published in "Yankee Doodle." 1846.   *New York Public Library*

[1846] MEDIATION AND PACIFICATION 62
    By E. W. Clay. *Lithograph. Published by H. R. Robinson.*
                                    American Antiquarian Society

[1846] THE MEXICAN COMMANDER ENJOYING THE PROSPECT OPPOSITE
         MATAMORAS 64
    Lithograph by Sarony & Major. Published by T. W. Strong.
                                    New York Historical Society

[1846] UNCLE SAM'S TAYLORIFICS 64
    By E. W. Clay. *Lithograph.*   *New York Historical Society*

[1848] JOSHUA COMMANDING THE SUN TO STAND STILL 66
    By W. F. C. *Lithograph. Published by H. R. Robinson.*
                                    New York Public Library

[1850] SLAVERY AS IT EXISTS IN AMERICA.—SLAVERY AS IT EXISTS IN
         ENGLAND 68
    Lithograph. Published by J. Haven, Boston.

[1851] PRACTICAL ILLUSTRATION OF THE FUGITIVE-SLAVE LAW . . . 70
    By E. C. *Lithograph.*   *New York Public Library*

[1854] THE "OSTEND DOCTRINE". PRACTICAL DEMOCRATS CARRYING
         OUT THE PRINCIPLE 72
    By Louis Maurer. *Lithograph. Published by Currier & Ives.*

[1856] FANCIED SECURITY, OR THE RATS ON A BENDER 74
    By Louis Maurer. *Lithograph. Published by Currier & Ives.*
                                    New York Public Library

[1856] THE GREAT REPUBLICAN REFORM PARTY CALLING ON THEIR
         CANDIDATE 76
    By Louis Maurer. *Lithograph. Published by Currier & Ives.*

[1856] LIBERTY, THE FAIR MAID OF KANSAS—IN THE HANDS OF THE
    "BORDER RUFFIANS" 78
    Lithograph.   *New York Public Library*

[1856] SOUTHERN CHIVALRY—ARGUMENT VERSUS CLUB'S 80
    By J. L. Magee. Lithograph.   *New York Public Library*

[1858] THE LITTLE GIANT—IN THE CHARACTER OF THE GLADIATOR . . 82
    Lithograph.   *New York Public Library*

[1860] GREAT MATCH AT BALTIMORE, BETWEEN THE "ILLINOIS"
    BANTAM AND THE "OLD COCK" OF THE WHITE HOUSE 84
    Lithograph. Published by Currier & Ives.   *New York Public Library*

[1860] "THE IRREPRESSIBLE CONFLICT." OR THE REPUBLICAN BARGE IN
    DANGER 86
    Lithograph. Published by Currier & Ives.   *American Antiquarian Society*

[1860] THE POLITICAL RAIL SPLITTER 86
    Lithograph. Published by J. Leach, New York.   *New York Public Library*

[1860] PROGRESSIVE DEMOCRACY.—PROSPECT OF A SMASH UP 88
    Lithograph. Published by Currier & Ives.   *New York Public Library*

[1860] THE NATIONAL GAME. THREE "OUTS" AND ONE "RUN."
    ABRAHAM WINNING THE BALL 90
    Lithograph. Published by Currier & Ives.   *American Antiquarian Society*

[1861] LITTLE BO-PEEP AND HER FOOLISH SHEEP 92
    Wood Engraving. Published by T. W. Strong.   *New York Public Library*

[1861] THE "SECESSION MOVEMENT" 94
    Lithograph. Published by Currier & Ives.   *American Antiquarian Society*

[1861] THE INSIDE TRACK 96
    By Henry L. Stephens. Published in "Vanity Fair," New York, March 2, 1861.
                                          New York Public Library

[1861] DARING LEAP 96
    By Henry L. Stephens. Published in "Vanity Fair," New York, March 16, 1861.
                                          New York Public Library

[1862] BREAKING THAT "BACKBONE" 98
    By Benjamin Day. Lithograph. Published by Currier & Ives.
                                          New York Public Library

[1862] DISSOLVING VIEWS OF RICHMOND 100
    No. 3 Lithograph.   *New York Public Library*

[1862] WORSHIP OF THE NORTH 100
    By Adalbert J. Volck ("Blada"). Etching.   *Whitney Museum of American Art*

[1864] THE GRAVE OF THE UNION, OR MAJOR JACK DOWNING'S DREAM 102
    Drawn by Zeke. Lithograph.   *New York Public Library*

[1864] COMPROMISE WITH THE SOUTH 104
    By Thomas Nast. Published in "Harper's Weekly," September 3, 1864.
                                          New York Public Library

[1864] OUR FOREIGN RELATIONS 106
    By A. Hochstein. Lithograph.   *New York Public Library*

[1864] RUNNING THE "MACHINE" 108
 Lithograph. Published by Currier & Ives.   *New York Public Library*

[1864] THE COMMANDER-IN-CHIEF CONCILIATING THE SOLDIER'S VOTES ON THE BATTLE FIELD 110
 Reproduction of pen drawing.   *New York Public Library*

[1868] "SPOONS" AS FALSTAFF MUSTERING THE IMPEACHMENT MANAGERS 112
 By Thomas Worth. *Lithograph. Published by John McDermott, New York.*
   New York Public Library

[1868] RECONSTRUCTION, OR A WHITE MAN'S GOVERNMENT 114
 Lithograph. Published by Currier & Ives.   *New York Public Library*

[1868] THE MAN OF WORDS. THE MAN OF DEEDS. WHICH DO YOU THINK THE COUNTRY NEEDS? 116
 Lithograph. Published by Currier & Ives.   *New York Public Library*

[1871] A GROUP OF VULTURES WAITING FOR THE STORM TO "BLOW OVER."—LET US "PREY." 118
 By Thomas Nast. *Published in "Harper's Weekly," Sept. 23, 1871.*
   New York Public Library

[1872] ADDING INSULT TO INJURY. ANYTHING TO MAKE OUR REPUBLIC LOOK RIDICULOUS 120
 By Thomas Nast. *Published in "Harper's Weekly," May 25, 1872.*
   New York Public Library

[1872] THE APPLE OF DISCORD AT THE GENEVA TRIBUNAL 122
 By Thomas Nast. *Published in "Harper's Weekly," Oct. 5, 1872.*
   New York Public Library

[1878] A PICTURE FOR OUR EMPLOYERS 124
 By Joseph Keppler. *Published in "Puck," Aug. 21, 1878.*
   New York Public Library

[1880] WELCOME TO ALL! 126
 By Joseph Keppler. *Published in "Puck," April 28, 1880.*
   New York Public Library

[1880] PUCK WANTS "A STRONG MAN AT THE HEAD OF GOVERNMENT"— BUT NOT THIS KIND 128
 By Joseph Keppler. *Published in "Puck," Feb. 4, 1880.*
   New York Public Library

[1880] "STRONG" GOVERNMENT 1869–77. "WEAK" GOVERNMENT 1877–80 130
 By James A. Wales. *Published in "Puck," May 12, 1880.*
   New York Public Library

[1880] FORBIDDING THE BANNS 132
 By Joseph Keppler. *Published in "Puck," Aug. 25, 1880.*
   New York Public Library

[1880] THE CINDERELLA OF THE REPUBLICAN PARTY 134
 By Joseph Keppler. *Published in "Puck," Oct. 13, 1880.*
   New York Public Library

[1881] A HARMLESS EXPLOSION 136
 By Joseph Keppler. *Published in "Puck," May 25, 1881.*
   New York Public Library

[1881] A Grand Shakesperian Revival Which We Have But Little
Hope of Seeing on the Stage of the National Capital . . 138
By Joseph Keppler. *Published in "Puck," Oct. 5, 1881.*
New York Public Library

[1882] The Modern Prometheus 140
By Bernhard Gillam. *Published in "Puck," Feb. 22, 1882.*

[1882] First Annual Pic-Nic of the "Knights of Labor" 142
By Joseph Keppler. *Published in "Puck," June 21, 1882.*
New York Public Library

[1882] Uncle Sam's Neglected Farm 144
By Joseph Keppler. *Published in "Puck," Aug. 23, 1882.*

[1884] The Writing on the Wall 146
By Joseph Keppler. *Published in "Puck," June 18, 1884.*
New York Public Library

[1884] The Blaine Tariff Fraud 148
By Thomas Nast. *Published in "Harper's Weekly," Nov. 1, 1884.*
New York Public Library

[1884] He Can't Beat His Own Record 148
By Joseph Keppler. *Published in "Puck," July 30, 1884.*
New York Public Library

[1885] Foes in His Path. The Herculean Task Before Our Next
President 150
By Bernhard Gillam. *Published in "Puck," Feb. 18, 1885.*
New York Public Library

[1885] No Welcome for the Little Stranger 152
By Eugene Zimmerman ("Zim"). *Published in "Puck," Oct. 21, 1885.*
New York Public Library

[1886] The Free-Trade Bugaboo 154
By Charles J. Taylor. *Published in "Puck," May 5, 1886.*
New York Public Library

[1886] The Real Struggle 156
By Joseph Keppler. *Published in "Puck," May 12, 1886.*
New York Public Library

[1887] The Opening of the Congressional Session 158
By Joseph Keppler. *Published in "Puck," Dec. 7, 1887.*
New York Public Library

[1888] The Goose That Lays the Golden Eggs 160
By Bernhard Gillam. *Published in "Judge," Sept. 8, 1888.*
New York Public Library

[1888] A Hydra That Must Be Crushed and the Sooner the Better 160
By Joseph Keppler. *Published in "Puck," March 7, 1888.*
New York Public Library

[1889] Bosses of the Senate 162
By Joseph Keppler. *Published in "Puck," Jan. 23, 1889.*
New York Public Library

[1889] A Cold Reception Everywhere 164
By Joseph Keppler. *Published in "Puck," July 3, 1889.*

[1889] ONE SLAVE AND MANY MASTERS 166
By Joseph Keppler. *Published in "Puck," Sept. 18, 1889.*
New York Public Library

[1890] "THE MINORITY BE D——D" 168
By Louis Dalrymple. *Published in "Puck," Feb. 5, 1890.*

[1890] NONE BUT MILLIONAIRES NEED APPLY.—THE COMING STYLE OF
PRESIDENTIAL ELECTION 170
By Joseph Keppler. *Published in "Puck," March 12, 1890.*

[1890] THE NATIONAL GRAB-BAG.—"HELP YOURSELF" 172
By Joseph Keppler. *Published in "Puck," April 16, 1890.*

[1890] THE RAVEN 174
By Joseph Keppler. *Published in "Puck," Aug. 13, 1890.*
New York Public Library

[1896] WILL IT RISE? 176
By F. Victor (i.e., Victor Gillam). *Published in "Judge," March 7, 1896.*
New York Public Library

[1896] POLITICAL PIRATES 178
By Charles J. Taylor. *Published in "Puck," Sept. 23, 1896.*
New York Public Library

[1896] A MAN OF MARK 180
By Homer C. Davenport. *Published in "N. Y. Journal," Aug. 4, 1896.*

[1897] THE TANTALUS OF TO-DAY 180
By J. S. Pughe. *Published in "Puck," June 2, 1897. New York Public Library.*

[1896] SHE IS GETTING TOO FEEBLE TO HOLD THEM 182
By J. S. Pughe. *Published in "Puck," Nov. 18, 1896. New York Public Library*

[1897] TIME NEARLY UP 182
By Joseph Keppler, Jr. *Published in "Puck," Oct. 13, 1897.*
New York Public Library

[1898] THE CARES OF A GROWING FAMILY 184
By J. Campbell Cory. *Published in "The Bee," May 25, 1898.*
New York Public Library

[1900] "YES WILLIE, NURSIE HAS HAD TO SIT ON TEDDY" 184
By Frederick B. Opper. *Published in "N. Y. Evening Journal."*

[1899] THE WHITTLER FOR THE WORLD 186
By F. Victor Gillam. *Published in "Judge," July 1, 1899.*
New York Public Library

[1900] DON QUIXOTE BRYAN MEETS DISASTER IN HIS FIGHT AGAINST
JUDGE'S "FULL DINNER PAIL" 188
By F. Victor Gillam. *Published in "Judge," Nov. 10, 1900.*
New York Public Library

[1902] TWENTY YEARS AFTER 190
By J. S. Pughe. *Published in "Puck," Nov. 19, 1902. New York Public Library.*

INTRODUCTION

THE GRATITUDE which more than one nation has felt toward an eminent cartoonist in time of crisis is expressed in statements such as that attributed to Lincoln—that Nast was his "best recruiting sergeant." Gillray lives in the caricatures which helped to put fierce determination into Napoleon's enemies. Nor is the cartoonist less useful in time of peace. John Tenniel was given knighthood for general artistic labors. But he would have earned it by four famous cartoons of 1890 alone. One, "Dropping the Pilot," showed the Kaiser dismissing Bismarck. One presented the Kaiser as Europe's enfant terrible, rocking the boat while France, Italy, and other nations implored him not to tempt fate. A third, dealing with the East Africa arrangement by which Germany got Helgoland as a bonus, depicted Salisbury as a complacent grocer handing the German stripling a candy rabbit, "given away with a pound of tea." The fourth warned Russia to halt her persecution of the Jews; the ghost of Pharaoh adjuring the Czar, who stood with sword "Persecution" over a prostrate Hebrew: "Forbear! That weapon always wounds the hand that wields it."

Caricature has various forms. The political cartoon in the nineteenth century, with which this volume deals, was the central type of caricature in America during most of that period. Political caricature in a young democracy is likely to precede social caricature. One can flourish in a new and immature country; the other cannot. In the field of letters we had passably good political satirists—Francis Hopkinson, John Trumbull, J. K. Paulding, Seba Smith—before we had good social satirists. Just so, we had effective cartoons upon public affairs long before any artist offered what Ruskin credited to John Leech, "the definition and natural history of our society, the kind and subtle analysis of its foibles." That came in due time, but the social structure had to develop in complexity before it was possible.

What are the requirements of a really good political cartoon? The first is wit or humor; this should be smart and flashing, not a mere broad comic effect obtained by exaggeration. An apt early example is the famous "Gerrymander" figure of 1812, erroneously attributed to Gilbert Stuart, but actually the work of Elkanah Tisdale. The Democrats had arbitrarily districted certain townships in Essex County, Massachusetts, to insure themselves a majority. By adding teeth, wings and claws to the outline of the area the artist produced a dragon of fearful mien, immortally ludicrous. Equally witty is Nast's cartoon published after the fiercely contested election of 1876. The Republican elephant, mutilated and bandaged, its honor in shreds after its dubious victory, disconsolately muses beside the grave of the Democratic donkey: "One more such Victory and I am undone." A fine spark of wit sometimes carries a cartoon into future political histories. That distinction awaited McCutcheon's "The Mysterious Stranger" in 1904. The political line-up, after Theodore Roosevelt had swept the country, showed the "Solid South"standing firm, represented by a fine old Southern gentleman; but all eyes were fixed on one soft-hatted, frock-coated figure, Missouri, which had crossed over to the "Republican Column" and stood self-conscious but determined.

The second requirement of a good cartoon is truth, or at least one side of the truth. The characters depicted must be instantly recognizable likenesses, personal idiosyncrasies not too heavily distorted. The situation presented must possess at least a rough fidelity to fact. To depict Lincoln as an awkward railsplitter was fair enough; to show him as a gorilla was a falsification from which men recoiled. When Nast portrayed Tweed as a fat man with a money-bag for a head—"the brains of the Tammany Ring"—he was truthful and savagely effective. When Homer Davenport drew the pudgy Mark Hanna with dollar-marks over his clothes he overstepped the mark. The *Nation* quite properly objected to a cartoon of Nast's in 1872 which conveyed the untrue idea that Schurz, Sumner, Trumbull and the Liberal Republicans were abandoning the Negro as they prepared to support an anti-Grant candidate for the Presidency. Entitled "The Boat's Crew that is going over: will Robinson Crusoe desert his Man Friday?" it showed Friday, the poor Negro, begging for support; Sumner a self-complacent Crusoe hurried by two crimps, Schurz and Fenton, into the boat "Cincinnati Convention"; and Greeley enthusiastically waving his hat toward the ship "Democracy," flying the Ku Klux banner. It was amusing but essentially false, and the cartoon has not lasted like those which present Nast's characteristic generosity and fairness.

The third requirement of a really great cartoonist is moral purpose. The monarchs of British and American caricature—Gillray, Leech, Tenniel, Nast, Keppler, Art Young, and others—were all men of strong convictions. It is such men who in the end have the deepest, most convincing influence. Artists of the stature of Nast and Keppler were able to take part in controlling the policy of the periodicals for which they drew, and to express their opinions freely. Nast had no hesitation at times in differing from the editor of *Harper's Weekly*, George William Curtis; just as later J. N. Darling ("Ding") had no hesitation in differing from newspapers which used his cartoons. Without moral earnestness no cartoonist is likely to give his work a quality of universality or permanency. Louis Philippe has been pretty well forgotten. But men are likely to remember how the Daumier school turned the heavy physiognomy of that fat-headed monarch into a symbol—*la poire*—of bourgeois stupidity. Tweed, Sweeny, Hall and Connolly were four local thieves who looted New York's treasury as local thieves have looted other cities. But Nast perpetuated these four men as types of greed and hypocrisy. We need such prodding at times, we of whom Mr. Dooley said: "As a people, Hinnissy, we're the greatest crusaders that iver was—f'r a short distance."

The subtly varied exercise of this art brings distortion, humor, satire to its aid. Sometimes the effect has been gained with a vigor almost brutal, sometimes with the delicacy of a waspish sting, or with good-humored raillery. The rapier may be used, the brickbat, the slapstick. But cheap humor of the obvious kind is not apt to appear in the highest type of political cartoon. The clown's bouncing bladder does not make the strong home-thrust.

Many pitfalls surround political caricature. One is intemperate partisanship, of the sort that Copperhead artists showed in drawing Lincoln, and that Gillam displayed in his abusive treatment of Cleveland in *Judge*. Another is overproduction. When a cartoonist drew but once a week, as for *Punch, Harper's,* or *Puck,* he had leisure for better work than when the daily journal expects something fresh every morning. American cartooning since 1890 has shown what Lowell called too many thoughts and too little thought. Inadequate artistry is also associated with newspaper production, for too many cartoonists never learn to draw properly. (Remember that Rowlandson and Daumier have long ago been accorded a place in artistic history, and no mean place at that.) A fourth defect frequently found in recent caricature is lack of principle. If we still have cartoonists of strong convictions, we have too many who put their faith at the disposal of the journal or syndicate which pays them. But though American caricature in our days has lacked any great dominating figure like Nast or Keppler, it has never been more abundant and varied, or perhaps of higher average quality.

The history of political cartooning in the United States during the nineteenth century might, with respect to media, be divided into four somewhat vaguely defined periods. The first was that of woodcuts and copper engravings, usually issued as separate publications. The second period, in which cartooning was far more varied and abundant, was ushered in by the establishment of commercial lithography. It began about 1830 and endured until well after the Civil War. Then began the era during which weekly publications reigned over the field, an era made illustrious by Nast, Keppler and Gillam. Finally, in the last fifteen years of the century, the daily newspaper became more and more the leader in presenting cartoons.

In the first of these four periods American cartoons were few and usually weak. It seems evident that the people had a natural taste for caricature. They had taken eagerly to the occasional lucky hits offered to them, such as Franklin's famous "Join or die" picture at the time of the French and Indian War and again before the Revolution—a snake cut into segments representing the Colonies. They had delighted in symbolic processions which were really a *caricature vivante*. When the new government was adopted in 1788, such processions showed the good ship *Constitution*, all sails set, rigging taut, and hull sound, in contrast to the old vessel *Confederation*, battered and woebegone. But in the rural republic it was difficult to find artists who could draw and engravers who could make plates. And in a land of thinly diffused population the market was poor and hard to reach. Yet some fair cartoons were produced by Tisdale, James Akin and Amos Doolittle, engravers who turned their hands to various jobs. The most famous of the early cartoonists was William Charles, a Scot driven from home because he had used his pencil too boldly, who worked in the tradition of Rowlandson and Gillray, and whose talents were spitefully employed against his native land during the War of 1812.

In these early cartoons liberal use was made of the allegorical style, and allegory is of necessity usually stilted, pompous, and deficient in humorous effect. Those cartoonists who adopted it—who showed Jefferson driven back by the American eagle as he was about to sacrifice the Constitution on the altar of Gallic despotism, or Liberty veiling her face as Satan and the British Lion incited Peter Porcupine (William Cobbett) to pour out his venomous articles—were trying to be grandiosely impressive, not incisive. Yet now and then they achieved a piquant effect. In 1807 Tisdale drew an admirably graphic plate, "Infant Liberty Nursed by Mother Mob." Its depiction of a greasy slut suckling an obstreperous cub upon whiskey and rum, while a mob attacks a public building, has true satiric edge.

When the early cartoonists deserted symbolism they were likely to become sadly literal, or at best to take refuge in an obvious pun. In the well-drawn plates on "Non-Intercourse" and "Intercourse," both signed "Peter Pencil," we get recognizable portraits of Jefferson, George III, and a still thin and youthful Napoleon. In the first the lanky Jefferson is reduced by his stoppage of American commerce to a shirt, breeches full of holes, and slippers. In the second, Napoleon and George III are robbing Jefferson, both well-armed and aggressive, while the defenseless President cowers in dismay. William Murrell correctly says that the greater part of the humorous drawing in America down to 1850 was simply a kind of "graphic reporting."

The period of greater productivity that came in with lithographing was more interesting. Partly because the Jacksonian era made for a great increase in all kinds of publications, partly because lithography was simple and inexpensive, cartoons soon poured out in a steady stream. For fifty years lithographed prints remained popular; about six hundred have been identified. Currier & Ives, among others, produced many, often taking both sides of a public question. The best of these lithographs had a simple naturalness, a direct candor, that is highly engaging, if only because it reflects a certain naivete in the public mind. They indicate the leisureness of the period; they were frequently cluttered with so many public figures, and contained so many speeches caught in curved loops, that it took time to puzzle out their full meaning. It is useless to look in these "omnibus" productions for such quickness of wit as Daumier or Leech offered, or for such truly comic exaggeration as in the best of Cruikshank. Very few of the artists had any qualities of the effective cartoonist; they offered statement of fact, or supposed fact, without strong emphasis in drawing. The artists also played much upon set ideas or conventional situations. A Presidential or gubernatorial canvass was a race of some kind, usually a steeplechase; a defeat was a voyage up Salt River, or a funeral. A contest between two political champions, after the great Heenan-Sayers fight, was a pugilistic bout. But despite the hackneyed nature of many such ideas, we must accord the work of the better cartoonists in this period a noteworthy place.

Take James Akin's cartoon "A Hickory Apology." We see Jackson, his gray locks bristling with anger, squaring away to attack the flustered Louis Philippe, whose government has declined to pay American claims on France. Behind the king a crowd of frogs sends up a chorus of expostulations; behind Jackson is a formidable fleet of warships. All very banal, yet highly amusing. The boastful note, truly American, is good-natured rather than malicious. Or take some of the cartoons of Edward Williams Clay, who brought to his work a fresh touch. His "Rats Leaving a Falling House" dealt with the breakup of Jackson's Cabinet after the Peggy Eaton scandal. Jackson is flabbergasted as his Cabinet, in the guise of rats with human heads, flee in all directions; he frantically clamps a foot on the tail of Van Buren. It was quite true that the widower remained after other Secretaries, whose wives objected to Peggy, had resigned. The cartoon hits off the situation neatly. Clay was an artist of ability, as appears from one of his lithographs, "The Times," reproduced in this volume. Other early artists in lithography who deserve mention were Napoleon Sarony and D. C. Johnston. The latter's "Symptoms of a Locked Jaw," depicting Henry Clay sewing up the mouth of Jackson, was a famous hit. Later came Louis Maurer, working for Currier & Ives, which firm brought out a varied and interesting array of cartoons upon the rising fever of the slavery issue, the Kansas question, and the campaigns of 1856 and 1860.

Like the lithographed print, the weekly humorous publication was borrowed from Europe. Philipon founded *Le Charivari* in Paris in 1832. London saw the first issue of that greatest of all humorous magazines, *Punch*, in 1841. The Germans followed with *Fliegende Blätter* of Munich in 1844 and *Kladderadatsch* of Berlin in 1848. But in the United States it was not until shortly before the Civil War that weekly publications began to afford caricature a new scope. To be sure, *Yankee Doodle* and *John Donkey* eked out brief careers at the end of the forties, the *Lantern* threw its glimmer over Millard Fillmore's two last years in the White House, and *Yankee Notions* held out from 1852 into the seventies. But the first magazine to establish itself firmly in political caricature was *Harper's Weekly*, founded in 1857. Then, in the fateful month of John Brown's raid, December 1859, *Vanity Fair* appeared; it did not last out the Civil War. But for a time it gave America a rival of the best humorous periodicals of Europe.

For three decades the weeklies held undisputed primacy. Before the Civil War was ended Nast had made *Harper's Weekly* a political power, his pencil wielding more influence than the pen of its editors. Though born in Bavaria, Nast found his best models in drawing and caricature in "the three great English Johns," Leech, Gilbert, and Tenniel. In 1862 he became a staff artist for *Harper's Weekly*, doing pictures of camp and battlefield. As the war progressed, he threw aside the illustrating of actual events, and strove to awaken the North to the deeper meaning of the conflict. The most powerful cartoon the country had yet seen came from his hand in the Presidential campaign of 1864. His "Compromise with the South," included in this volume, appeared just after the Democratic Convention in Chicago had declared the war a failure and called for a negotiated peace. Showing a triumphant Southerner shaking hands with a mutilated and dejected Northern veteran across the grave of Union soldiers fallen in a useless war, while Columbia weeps at the headstone, it was reprinted in millions of copies as a campaign document. That drawing remains one of the most eloquent indictments of appeasers ever put upon paper.

Nast remained a national power for the next quarter-century. He was not always on the right side. In the battle over Reconstruction he bitterly attacked Johnson as King Andy I, ranging himself with the intemperate Radicals under Thaddeus Stevens and Charles Sumner. During the Grant Administration he stuck by the confused President through thick and thin, palliating prevalent corruption and treating Greeley in 1872 with merciless scorn. He was deeply suspicious of the Catholic Church, and sought to keep alive old prejudices against it. But in two critical situations he served the country well. Almost the first to assail municipal corruption in post-war New York, for a time he fought the Tweed Ring almost singlehanded, and probably did more than all other leaders and journals to bring about its overthrow. The great cartoon "The Tammany Tiger loose—What are you going to do about it?"—Tweed gazing arrogantly from his seat as the tiger in the arena tears the Republic to pieces—still has power to thrill. And when in 1884 Reform found its champion in Grover Cleveland, Reaction in James G. Blaine, the cartoonist, by his attacks on the plumed knight, made thousands of voters regard the Republican candidate as an impostor and fraud. Nast's powerful imagination gave him striking skill in the use of symbolism. He permanently stamped upon the mind of the country those felicitous inventions, the Democratic donkey, the Republican elephant, and the Tammany tiger. No artist, in a period replete with literary allusions, made more frequent or effective use of Shakespeare; he drew upon Aesop, Cervantes, the Arabian Nights, and a wide range of other writings with equal happiness. His portraits were so good that anyone who leafs through Albert Bigelow Paine's life of Nast will find there the best picture-gallery of American politics between 1865 and 1890. For skill, fecundity, variety, *vis comica*, generous good nature, and idealism, he stands at the front among America's caricaturists, and among the best half-dozen in the world. And there are not too many of the best, after all.

Harper's Weekly always had rivals. Many caricatures appeared in *Frank Leslie's Weekly;* William Newman and Matt Morgan, both Englishmen, and Keppler, drew for it. And presently the country was given a novelty in the brightly tinted lithographic cartoons of *Puck* and *Judge.* Joseph Keppler, Viennese artist and actor, in 1869 established in St. Louis an illustrated weekly, *Die Vehme,* succeeded next year by his short-lived *Puck,* also in the German tongue, though a part-English text was soon supplied. In New York, in September, 1876, he issued the first number of a new German-language *Puck,* and the following March gave it an English edition. With a marked comic gift, genuine artistic capacity, and a keen flair for politics, Keppler quickly made his journal a success.

These weeklies (to which we should add *Life,* founded in 1883) gradually drove the lithographic prints of the old days out of existence. The political cartoons of Currier & Ives and their like had suited a nation of villages and small cities. But as *Harper's, Leslie's, Puck, Judge, Life,* and other weeklies attained a huge total circulation, these journals monopolized the field. The cartoons of Nast, Keppler, and Bernhard Gillam were artistically superior to the old work. Many of them still contained large groups of figures and often presented elaborate situations, but they were carefully drawn and composed. Keppler and Gillam, like Nast, had a wonderful eye for expression, and gave speaking likenesses of prominent politicians. The cartoons at their best had imagination and grace as well as trenchantly vigorous satire. Such crudities as the loops for quotations, and the involved explanatory text below, were discarded; the scene was so conceived that the picture told its story with instant effect. By the time of the exciting Mugwump campaign of 1884, with Keppler, Nast and Gillam taking Cleveland's side while *Judge* (for which Gillam later did strongly anti-Cleveland drawings) took Blaine's, the great cartoonists swayed many voters.

It was in this campaign that daily journalism scored its first tremendous hit in cartooning. When Blaine, just before election day, attended the glittering dinner arranged by Levi P. Morton for Jay Gould, Russell Sage, W. H. Vanderbilt, and other plutocrats, the New York *World* published Walt McDougall's cartoon "The Royal Feast of Belshazzar," and made history. This depiction of the money-kings feasting on monopoly pudding and lobby pie while the poor man begged in vain for a crust—though poor enough as a drawing—wrought a great impression. Cartoons had previously been used in the seventies and eighties by the New York *Daily Graphic.* As the century entered its last decade, they became common in the dailies. The retirement of Nast from *Harper's Weekly* in 1886, and the death of Keppler in 1894, helped to open the way. Moreover, the establishment of a livelier, spicier, more vigorously crusading journalism under Pulitzer and Hearst involved a wider use of pictures.

Soon every important daily, with few exceptions, had its cartoonist. Little by little their work crowded the more careful cartoons of the weeklies to the wall, for they took up every striking new issue as soon as it broke, and thus robbed it of all freshness before a weekly comment could be printed. The conditions under which daily cartoons were drawn required a return to simplicity. Elaborate group-scenes became uncommon, and the lines often combined crudity with dash and vigor. High salaries were paid to men who could supply cleverness, fertility, and force; the names of cartoonists who could meet some or all of these requirements—John T. McCutcheon, Frederick B. Opper, Charles G. Bush, Homer Davenport, Charles R. Macauley—became household words by 1900 or soon after. *Harper's Weekly*, *Life*, *Puck*, and *Judge* tried valiantly to carry on. In W. A. Rogers *Harper's* found a cartoonist of more finish than power; *Judge* lost Bernhard Gillam by death in 1896 and somewhat inadequately replaced him by his brother Victor and others; *Life* had William H. Walker who bravely opposed the Spanish War and the Imperialist fever. But the daily press not only drained away the circulation of the weeklies, but took some of their artists as well.

American cartooning has naturally flourished best when great political issues and figures held the nation's attention. The stormy administrations of Jefferson and Madison, culminating in the War of 1812, produced far more pictorial satire than the periods which immediately preceded and followed them. From 1817 to 1829, that so-called "era of good feelings" which was really an era of petty squabbling, practically no cartoons of merit can be found. But the imperious figure of Jackson, and the angry feeling created by his policies and by the panic of 1837, gave caricature a powerful stimulus. The Mexican War period again saw some telling hits at various figures and measures, as well as expressions of spread-eagle exultation in Manifest Destiny. The slavery controversy, despite a depressing tendency at first to evade the central issue, by 1856 generated a great deal of earnest conviction. The Civil War, Reconstruction, Civil Service Reform, the Mugwump revolt, Populism, Free Silver, the tariff battles of 1890 and 1894, the Spanish War and Imperialism all called forth a heavy quota of cartoons. Those leaders who had some quality of picturesqueness lent themselves best to cartooning. Not necessarily great men, but such as possessed thrust and color. Jackson, Lincoln and Theodore Roosevelt were of course prime favorites of the cartoonist. But pugnacious Stephen A. Douglas, strutting Roscoe Conkling, enigmatic S. J. Tilden, hawklike Blaine, stalwart Cleveland were all also much employed. A colorless man like Hayes was passed over, unless his very colorlessness could be satirized, as in "Benny" Harrison lost under his grandfather's big hat.

Economic issues appeared late in caricature, as they did also in Congressional legislation. To the end of the nineteenth century no sharply radical notes were struck by the major cartoonists. "Monopoly," as it appeared in drawings of the thirties and forties, meant simply the monopoly of specially chartered banks, railroads, and canal companies. The Homestead question crops out in some cartoons of the fifties, but never, apparently, in connection with unemployment and low wages. Labor organizations and labor conflicts were long given a wide berth by the lithographers; when the weeklies took up these problems, it was in drawings which pointed out how much better conciliation was than battle, and warned the workingman against wily agitators. In the eighties the trusts began to appear as horrid monsters. The control of the Senate by huge corporations is condemned. But no cartoonist proposed government ownership of railroads, none strongly supported the Interstate Commerce Commission when it was first defied, and none offered really constructive suggestion on the trusts. The important cartoonists unanimously ridiculed Populism, and nearly all were sternly hostile to free silver. Even mildly Socialistic views would have to be sought in the files of the radical foreign language press. All this was natural enough, for America was a conservative country.

Despite their limitations American cartoons are invaluable to the student of political history. They bring us to face to face with a vast variety of political manoeuvrings, from Federalist opposition to the theories of the French Revolution down to the expedients of Mark Hanna and other standpatters for defeating change. They throw light on changes in national mood, now exhibiting our Jefferson Brick boastfulness as "the biggest nation in all creation," determined (till we backed down) upon "fifty-four-forty or fight," now showing the pusillanimity with which great sections of the population treated slavery and disunion. They present in vivid terms many a half-forgotten episode—the Hartford Convention, the Seminole War, the New Orleans massacre, the Star Route frauds. They recall the burning heat once generated by issues that are now extinct volcanoes: the Bank question, which made Clay men and Jacksonians mortal enemies; filibustering, which set Southerners against Northerners; Civil Service Reform, which put Stalwarts and Half-Breeds at one another's throats. They illuminate changing aspects of the Indian and tariff problems, two sempiternal concerns of the nation. They show how party spirit rose and ebbed, and reveal the artificiality of many party differences.

Along with all this, cartoons are singularly useful in portraying the spell which various personalities have cast over the public mind. Tom Reed cuts no great figure in history; but what a part he plays in cartoons from 1885 to 1900—a part eloquent of his place in the popular eye. Frémont, apart from his valuable explorations, had but a passing renown; but how the cartoons of 1856 bring out his motley following and the flaming idealism his cause awoke among Republicans! The speeches carried in the loops or balloons of the old cartoons are often as revealing as those of actual statesmen. Much social history, too, is bound up in the political caricatures of the past. Costumes of gentlemen and ladies, slave-drivers and Bowery "b'hoys"; furniture of bygone days; popular songs, colloquialisms, and slang of the past; the use made of slogans, transparencies, banners, and other political devices; fashions in food, drink, and tobacco; street-scenes of city and village—these are all evoked in the old prints. We see in cartoons, too, some of the folklore of former generations, as in the development of the symbolic figures of Brother Jonathan and Uncle Sam.

Evidently, the political cartoon is a valuable item in the documentary outfit of the historian. The laugh-provoker of yesterday has become a serious contribution to history.

Into changing times the great tradition of caricature marches on; a tradition that runs back to Hogarth and Rowlandson, nay, to ancient Egypt, and will doubtless die only when the human race dies. We have American cartoonists today who need take no shame in comparison with their predecessors. Rollin Kirby, Boardman Robinson, Daniel R. Fitzpatrick, William Gropper, J. N. Darling—these are but half of those who might be named. We look at their work with a lively sense of the controversial nature of present-day issues. Our emotions are strongly enlisted for or against the ideas they present. But when we turn back to this sheaf of nineteenth century cartoons, we have a different feeling. The roar of conflict, the heat of argument, the sting of unjust vituperation, have faded away; faces of dead men and symbols of dead issues may be regarded with serenity and quiet. Only the history remains—a type of history unique in piquancy of flavor and in its combination of the amusing and the instructive.

A CENTURY OF
POLITICAL CARTOONS

THE PROVIDENTIAL DETECTION

ANONYMOUS

[Probably 1800]

THE FRENCH REVOLUTION, and the ensuing wars between Britain and France, aroused the bitterest party feeling in the United States. When President Washington fixed upon neutrality as the proper course, partisans of France assailed him angrily. John Adams has told, in somewhat exaggerated terms, of "the terrorism excited by Genet in 1798, when ten thousand people in the streets of Philadelphia, day after day, threatened to drag Washington out of his house, and effect a revolution in the Government, or compel it to declare war in favor of the French Revolution and against England." Difficulties between the American and French governments had increased when the Washington administration in 1795 concluded the Jay treaty with Great Britain. When Adams sent a special mission of three men to Paris in 1797 to negotiate an agreement, Talleyrand insulted them by demanding a bribe, and by attempting to divide the Republican member, Elbridge Gerry, from his Federalist associates Pinckney and Marshall. This "X.Y.Z." affair aroused further indignation in America, and the year 1798 witnessed a brisk though undeclared naval war between French and American ships in the North Atlantic. Fortunately, Adams sent a second mission to France, and it restored peace, but could not wholly restore good feeling.

Upon Jefferson, recognized head of the party friendly to France, a heavy storm of opprobrium and denunciation was concentrated. He was identified in the eyes of his antagonists with the worst features of the French Revolution: intolerance, bloodshed, hostility to Christianity, general license and lawlessness. The commercial groups and moneyed elements of the North were generally favorable to Jay's Treaty and to Great Britain; they attacked Jefferson as an advocate of social disorder and of "levelling" tendencies. The clergy were suspicious of Jefferson's Deism; many were offended by his long fight against State support of religion in Virginia. It was well known that Jefferson had not been at all shocked by Shays' Rebellion; he thought a little rebellion now and then a good thing.

In this rather well drawn caricature all the venom of the opponents of Jefferson is concentrated. The Republican leader is kneeling before the snake-encircled "Altar of Gallic Despotism," dropping the letter to Mazzei which proved very damaging to its writer. In a burst of indiscretion, in 1796, Jefferson had written his Italian friend, Philip Mazzei, that while the mass of the American people were democratic, the government was reactionary. A vigorous fight would have to be waged, he declared, to preserve the liberties of the republic. The letter was printed in a Paris newspaper in 1798. Naturally, its attack on Washington as unfriendly to "republican principles" aroused resentment, and a great ado was made over the unhappy missive.

MAD TOM IN A RAGE

ANONYMOUS
[1801]

Party warfare of Federalists and Republicans engendered the utmost bitterness, and caricaturists used as much license as pamphleteers and newspaper editors. To show Jefferson as a madman and drunkard leagued with the devil in pulling down the Federal Government was not going too far for the robust taste of the period. In his admirable first inaugural address, Jefferson pledged himself to preserve the national government "in its whole Constitutional vigor." But the two parties were divided by an impassable chasm in ideas of what the Constitution meant. Under Washington and Adams the Federalists had established numerous precedents for far-reaching exercise of national authority. The government, with Hamilton as guide, had taken strong measures to establish national credit, suppressed the Whiskey Rebellion, braved the anger of the public in making a wise treaty with Great Britain, and passed the Alien and Sedition laws, which carried Federal police authority to an extreme point. Jefferson wished to reduce the powers of the Federal Government; he said so in his inaugural. Those who believed that national safety depended upon Federal vigor feared he would tear down the structure reared by the two first presidents. Actually, Jefferson was destined to stretch national authority to new limits, in extraordinary invasions of what had been deemed the rights of states and individuals. The Louisiana Purchase, the Non-Intercourse Act, and the Embargo all flew in the teeth of his original theories.

SEE PORCUPINE, IN COLOURS JUST PORTRAY'D

ANONYMOUS
[1799]

That doughty Englishman, William Cobbett, coming to the United States in 1792, set up *Porcupine's Gazette* in Philadelphia in 1797. He was a staunch supporter of the Adams Administration. His policy, pro-English and anti-French, at first accorded with Adams's views. Giving "two blows for one," as he said, Cobbett, one of the most trenchant writers of English prose, was more than a match for Republican editors like William Duane. Here he appears as a porcupine, encouraged by the devil, who calls for "more scandal," and by the British lion, decorated with a ribbon representing Jay's Treaty. Liberty weeps on a medallion head of Franklin. The cartoon probably pleased Cobbett, who found his element in battle.

THE CAT LET OUT OF THE BAG

BY WILLIAM CHARLES

[1808]

Vigorous efforts had to be made by Jefferson's supporters to counteract the uproar of the Federalists over the Embargo. This law of December, 1807, laid a heavy hand on the economic life of the country. No vessels might depart for any foreign port, and coastwise ships had to post bonds that they would land their cargoes in home ports. Thousands of sailors were thrown out of work; shipbuilders closed their yards; import merchants went into bankruptcy. Before long the farmer was hard hit, for the closing of the foreign markets created a glut, and prices fell precipitously. Naturally the anti-Jeffersonian press made the most of this disastrous situation. New England was suffering heavily. Except for one State, Connecticut, that section had gone Republican in 1804, but now it was preparing to return to the Federalist banner—and, except for little Vermont, in 1808 did so.

Charles's well-conceived but badly drawn cartoon insists that true American sailors think of patriotism first, and of safety and prosperity second—thus teaching a lesson to all their countrymen. Three sturdy tars are taking their dram and discussing the news; one with a copy of the Embargo Act before him, another with the latest British Order in Council. When they are accosted by a ragged little Federalist editor, carrying under his arm a ledger labelled "Boston Gazette Account With Great Britain," their scorn is unbounded. He urges them to resist the Embargo, to do nothing to displease the mother country, good old England. But they are ready to face impressment, British prisons, war, or any other hard knocks; for "who would mutiny 'gainst commander and desert ship 'cause a hard gale and a tough passage brings him to short allowance?" The *Gazette* here arraigned was the *Commercial Gazette*, later *Russell's Gazette*, which along with the *Columbian Centinel* upheld the Federalist opposition to Jefferson's measures and "Mr. Madison's War." Back of the editor there pours out of the "Tory Cave" a swarm of other Federalist sheets, each in the guise of an ape: the Norfolk *Ledger*, the Charleston *Courier*, the New York *(Commercial) Gazette*, and many more.

In the second state of this plate, its title was changed to "The Tory Editor and His Apes Giveing Their Pitiful Advice to American Sailors." When it was drawn, William Charles had but recently arrived from England. Of the two dozen American cartoons which he issued 1807–1817, most deal with the War of 1812. The work of this artist was in the British tradition, and proved very popular. Though he unblushingly borrowed ideas from Gillray, he had a lumbering force of his own, and his death in 1820 was a real blow to American cartooning.

JOHN BULL MAKING A NEW BATCH OF SHIPS TO SEND TO THE LAKES

BY WILLIAM CHARLES
[1814]

For the British to lose their fleet on Lake Erie in 1813 to the youthful Oliver Hazard Perry was bad enough; their loss of a squadron on Lake Champlain the following year to Captain Thomas Macdonough was worse. This squadron was essential to the invasion of New York by Sir George Prevost's army. When in the battle of Plattsburg Bay every British ship was either sunk or captured, Prevost had to march back to Canada without striking a blow. The consolation of the British was that they had command of the high seas, and were able to drive American shipping from the ocean and transport their armies along the coast at will. But in holding this command they suffered numerous small losses, of which one is mentioned in this caricature—the victory of the Yankee *Fox* over the *Stranger*.

Charles's cartoon was obviously inspired by Gillray's masterly work on Napoleon setting up his puppet-thrones: "Tiddy-Doll, the great French Gingerbread-Baker, drawing out a New Batch of Kings." But Charles had his own sense of humor. His conception of John Bull (apparently a medley of John Bull and King George) spluttering "What—what—what!" is excellent. Another cartoon, relating to Yankee naval victories, "Queen Charlotte and Johnny Bull get their Dose of Perry," carries a punning reference to Perry the victor and perry the drink of pear juice. Bull, obviously suffering from severe gastric disturbances, laments that he has had a bad overdose. The same pun is implied in Amos Doolittle's "Brother Jonathan administering a salutary cordial to John Bull" (1813), the cordial being "Perry."

Among Charles's other cartoons on the War of 1812, two furnish interesting comment on American naval and military activities. One, "Johnny Bull and the Alexandrians" (reproduced in this volume), shows the conquering Briton in his march on Washington asking for flour, tobacco, and other stores —all except "Porter and Perry—I've had enough of them already." A British soldier remarks: ". . . the Yankees are not all so cowardly as these fellows here—let's make the best of our time." In the second cartoon, "John Bull and the Baltimoreans," Bull meets an opposition which quite disconcerts him. A triumphant American rifleman cries: "Oh hoh—Johnny, you thought you had Alexandrians to deal with." In August, 1814, the British had marched into Washington and British officers had eaten a meal prepared at the White House for President Madison; but the assertion of General Ross that he would spend the winter in Baltimore proved ill-founded when the British fleet was repulsed before Fort McHenry, and Ross himself was killed by a rifleman.

JOHNNY BULL AND THE ALEXANDRIANS
BY WILLIAM CHARLES
[1815]

CHARLES DEPICTS THE British invaders as arrogant pillagers, and the citizens of Alexandria as weak-kneed caitiffs. Both indictments were overdrawn. When the British army under Ross captured Washington, a naval force under Captain Gordon pushed up the Potomac, took Fort Washington and held the town of Alexandria to ransom. Some ships and stores were handed over to him. The British then voyaged down the river to Chesapeake Bay without meeting real resistance. The poor Alexandrians could hardly be blamed for yielding to the enemy demands after their defensive forces had been scattered. Nor could the British in Washington or Alexandria properly be accused of looting. The troops were kept under rigid control, private property in the capital was respected, and requisitions made in Alexandria were permitted by the rules of war. But Charles's cartoon was effective propaganda, skilfully planned to arouse hatred against the British and scorn of cowards. Nor did it fail to express the nation's pride in Commodore Perry and in Captain David Porter, whose ship *Essex* inflicted so much damage on the British merchant marine before she was captured by a superior force.

JOHN BULL BEFORE NEW ORLEANS
BY WILLIAM CHARLES
[1815]

HERE JOHN BULL is a thick-bodied lout, his wig and arms gone, his clothes disordered, being haled out of the swamps at New Orleans by an American rifleman and a Franco-American supporter. Well might the Americans crow over the victory that Jackson's army had won on January 8th, 1815. It almost wiped out the many failures which had preceded it. The British veterans of the Napoleonic campaigns had done all that brave soldiers could do. But they met what Sir Harry Smith called "the most murderous and destructive fire of all arms ever poured upon a column." The Americans failed at Bladensburg largely because they had no leader; they succeeded at New Orleans because they had a determined, inspiring captain, who made their patriotism and strength effective. The battle was fought more than a fortnight after peace had been made in Ghent, but it was not fought in vain. As the Americans had learned the difficulties and risks of invasion in their attempt on Canada, so the British learned these difficulties in the attempt on New Orleans.

THE HARTFORD CONVENTION, OR LEAP NO LEAP

BY WILLIAM CHARLES

[1815]

"To leap or not to leap"—Charles has hit off the mood of the Hartford Convention very well. Three States, Massachusetts, Connecticut, and Rhode Island, had sent delegates to meet in Hartford in December, 1814; they were joined by two men from New Hampshire and one from the town of Windham, Vermont. Discontent over the heavy reverses suffered in the war was one motive of the gathering. Most New Englanders had been against the conflict from the beginning, and the failure of the national arms confirmed them in their opposition. But they had other causes of resentment as well. They feared that the South and West would rule the nation permanently, and in a spirit hostile to the Northeast; agriculture would be promoted at the expense of commerce. Moreover, they were tired of the Virginia dynasty. Three Presidents out of four had come from the Old Dominion, and another was soon to be chosen. Why not break up the Union and form a new confederacy?

This was the demand of Timothy Pickering in particular. Secretary of State under Adams, then Senator, then Representative, Pickering ever since the purchase of Louisiana had feared that New England faced ruin. The new areas, fast filling up with settlers, would press measures hostile to the commercial section. He constantly wrote to his friends urging the erection of a Northern confederacy—a peaceable separation. In time he won a good many adherents. But when the Hartford Convention met, the moderate majority, guided by Harrison Gray Otis of Boston, stood firm against rash action. Instead, they protested against unconstitutional acts of Congress and "the abuses of bad administrations." In the end the convention contented itself with proposing seven amendments to the Constitution; one limiting the power of Congress to declare war, another making it harder to admit new States, and so on.

Charles shows Massachusetts, Connecticut, and little Rhode Island all shrinking from a step that presented too many risks. Great Britain, which hoped for the return of New England to the Empire, is shown tempting them by trade advantages and titles. Bald Pickering himself, who came from Essex County in Massachusetts, is praying that the movement will succeed; it will convert him from a plain Representative into "my lord of Essex." To shame these malcontents, a tablet on the New England rock is inscribed with the names of the heroes of the War of 1812.

The volume of lampoons, caricatures, and diatribes launched against the Hartford Convention soon made it a synonym for infamy. Because the Federalist Party was identified with its allegedly treasonable aims, the party, weakened by a variety of other circumstances, soon passed out of existence.

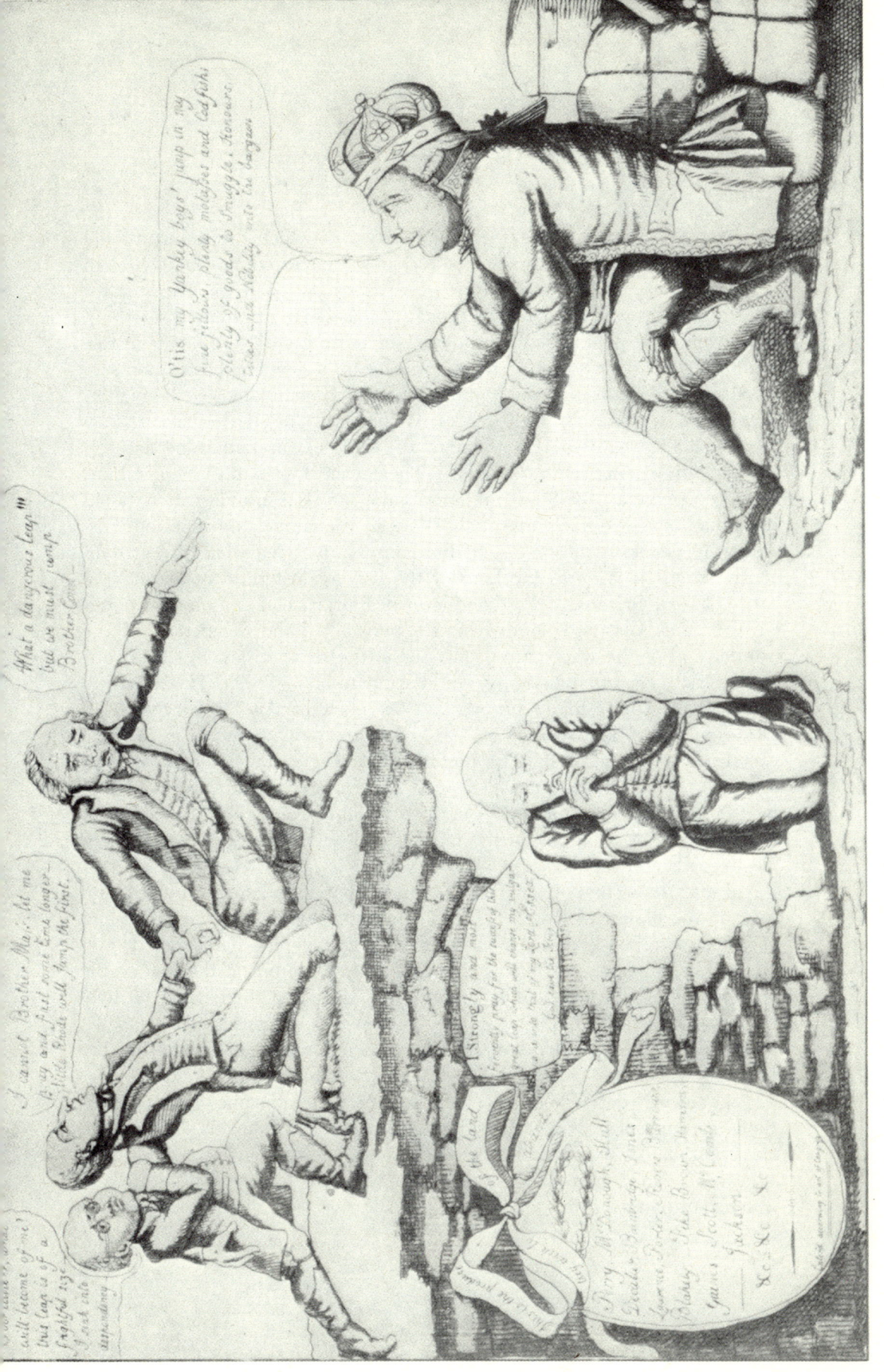

A FOOT-RACE

BY DAVID CLAYPOOLE JOHNSTON
[1824]

THE CAMPAIGN OF 1824 is one of the two in which the failure of the electoral college to choose a President transferred the final vote to the House of Representatives. It was exceptionally interesting for other reasons as well. The Congressional caucus having become discredited as an agency for nominating candidates, the State Legislatures stepped forward as agencies for selecting them. This meant a new emphasis upon sectionalism in the canvass. John Quincy Adams was nominated by the legislatures of various New England States; William H. Crawford of Georgia by the Virginia legislature; Henry Clay by the Kentucky and other legislatures, and Jackson by the Tennessee house. These were four strong men. Adams had been Secretary of State under Monroe, and his training in national affairs had been extremely thorough. His ability, courage, and conscientiousness were generally admired, and the conservatives regarded him as eminently "safe." Jackson as the hero of the war against the Creeks and the battle of New Orleans, and as conqueror of Florida, had an immense popularity in the West and Southwest. He personified the democracy of the frontier and of the wage-earning masses in the rising cities. But the word "safe" was the last that anybody would apply to him. William H. Crawford, who had been minister to France and Secretary of the Treasury, was an astute politician, and seemed on the highroad to victory when in 1823 he was stricken with paralysis. Clay had been Speaker, and was one of the most effective orators of the time. He stood for a more definite program than Jackson or Crawford—for the "American system," combining protection of manufactures by generous tariffs, and internal development by government aid to roads and canals.

The cartoon shows Clay pulling up in despair as Adams, Crawford, and Jackson run almost neck and neck. Old John Adams, waving a cocked hat, cheers on his "son Jack"; a Westerner with a stovepipe hat in hand cries "Hurra for our Jack*son*." It was true that Clay came out at the rear of the contest, but not so far behind Crawford as the artist indicates. The final result in the electoral college stood: Jackson 99, Adams 84, Crawford 41, and Clay 37. Jackson alone of the four received a truly national vote; the other three had only a sectional following. The House chose Adams.

At an early date a horse-race, or a foot-race, became one of the conventional methods of treating a Presidential canvass. But Johnston, "the American Cruikshank," was an artist of sufficient originality to give freshness even to a rather banal idea. His picture is marked by tolerant good-nature and absence of partisanship.

A NEW MAP OF THE UNITED STATES WITH THE ADDITIONAL TERRITORIES

PRINTED BY ANTHONY IMBERT

[1829]

LASHED TAIL TO TAIL, the Jacksonian Party of the West, represented by a voracious alligator, and the John Quincy Adams Party of the East, typified by an immobile tortoise, stretch across the entire Union—a Union to which are now attached the organized Territories of Florida, Michigan, and Arkansas, and a great unorganized Territory north and west of Missouri. The use of the alligator to symbolize the Western Democracy is interesting. A song of the time, "The Hunters of Kentucky," celebrated the prowess of the backwoods Kentuckians and Tennesseans, "half horse, half alligator," with whose aid Jackson had won the Battle of New Orleans. (Henry Clay rides such a nondescript animal in E. W. Clay's cartoon "Great American Steeple Chase for 1844," in which Calhoun is mounted on the "Nullification Coota Turtle.") As for the party of Adams, it had seemed sufficiently tortoise-like to most Americans.

In the election just concluded when this cartoon was issued, Jackson had swept the entire West and South, divided the Middle States with Adams, and, reaching up into Maine, carried one elector even there. The total electoral vote stood Jackson 178, Adams 83. A veritable revolution had occurred. The plain man, whether western farmer or eastern mechanic, had come into power with a hero who intensely disliked the moneyed and commercial classes of the great eastern cities. Such aristocrats as Josiah Quincy, here referred to as a handicap to Adams in his race, were henceforth to count for less in American affairs.

The figures standing atop the two party emblems are uttering some of the political catch-phrases of the day. One, for example, ejaculates "Coffin Handbills"—for the execution of eight Tennessee militiamen in Jackson's command, after due court-martial, had been recalled in 1828, as appears in the next cartoon in this book, by the issuance of handbills bearing crude pictures of coffins. But more interesting than these trivial hits are the Winnebago Indians at the top of the design. A party of them had recently visited the East. They are depicted here as returning to their less tutored fellows with some amusing impressions. One has seen the ballet-dancers, and can "teach our squaws now how to show their legs without any impropriety." Others have acquired enough English to say "A-dam No-a! Jack-son Ou-rah!"

This amateurish effort is supposed to be the first cartoon lithographed in America, and it is poor enough in execution, depending for its effect on the text scattered over the picture.

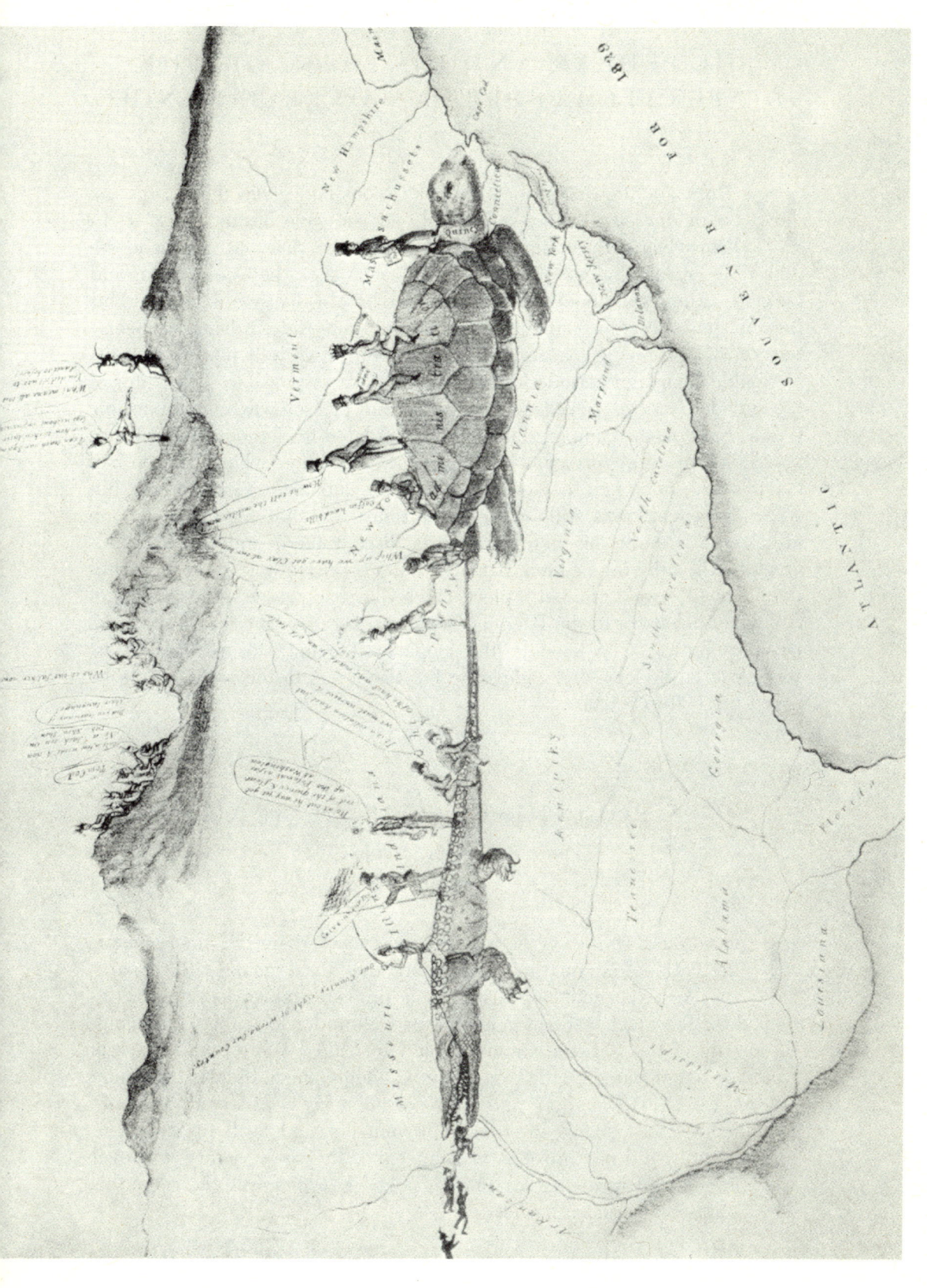

THE PEDLAR AND HIS PACK, OR THE DESPERATE EFFORT, AN OVER BALANCE
[1828]

By 1828, abolition of property qualifications had given the masses the ballot; increased interest in public affairs gave desire to use it. In Pennsylvania three times as many votes were cast that year as in the preceding Presidential election. When the voters chose between Adams and Jackson, "King Numbers" gave the popular hero a decisive majority. This cartoon shows three prominent figures on the losing side, Adams, his Secretary of State Henry Clay, and editor John Binns, while it hits off the discreditable campaign episode for which Binns was responsible. The editor of the Philadelphia *Democratic Press* believed that Jackson was an irresponsible tyrant. Early in the campaign he widely circulated his famous "coffin handbills," pictures of eight coffins bearing names of soldiers whom Jackson had commanded shot when they quit service at the end of their enlistments, but while the enemy was still in the field. Binns overshot his mark. A mob attacked his house; his newspaper was discontinued; and the handbills created sympathy for Jackson. Adams, vainly trying to hold on to his Presidential chair, speaks of a pet project which Clay had pressed—the sending of American delegates to the Panama Congress of Latin-American States proposed by Bolivar. Clay laments "the people are too much for us." Adams lost to Jackson in the electoral college by 178 to 83, and in the popular vote by about 650,000 to 500,000.

A POLITICAL GAME OF BRAG
PUBLISHED BY H. R. ROBINSON
[1831]

The presidential canvass for 1832 was marked by the emergence of the national nominating convention. Our first organized third party, the Anti-Masonic, appearing as a protest against secret societies, named for President William Wirt. It was well understood that Clay would be captain of the National Republicans, later called Whigs, while Jackson would be renominated by the Democrats. Calhoun here is a fourth contender, holding cards "Nullification" and "Anti-Tariff." Clay's "American System"—continuance of the Bank, internal improvements, and tariff protection for manufactures—did not prove a winning hand. Jackson's victory was overwhelming. Brag was the early name for poker, but obviously the game then had a phraseology that it has lost.

DESPOTISM—ANARCHY—DISUNION

ANONYMOUS

[1833]

THIS IS AN ATTEMPT at symbolism in the grand manner. Issued at the height of the Nullification crisis, it shows John C. Calhoun mounting the steps which lead from the Nullification Ordinance through treason, civil war, and disunion to anarchy. The glittering prize ahead of him is "Despotism"—the right to rule South Carolina, or perhaps a Southern Confederacy, unchecked. At one side, cheering him on, is James Henry Hammond of South Carolina, with epaulets and spurs. Hammond was tirelessly active in the military preparations which accompanied the nullification movement. He made fiery speeches, raised volunteers, and was chosen colonel of a regiment from the Barnwell District. On the other side, also urging Calhoun to push a little farther, is Governor Robert Y. Hayne. He had resigned from the Senate in order to give Vice President Calhoun a chance to enter that body, and as head of the State he defended its policy valiantly. When Jackson issued a proclamation denying the right of one State to nullify a law of the Federal Government, Hayne issued his own proclamation in reply—and it is here shown sticking out of his pocket. As commander-in-chief of his pugnacious little State, he summoned it to furnish ten thousand armed men to fight back any invader.

The cartoonist was justified in picturing Jackson as ready to hang a few traitors in order to stop disunion. When the South Carolina Convention on November 19, 1832, declared the tariffs of 1828 and 1832 null and void, and forbade Federal officers to collect any revenue under them in the State, the President was ready to snatch up the gauntlet. He sent a considerable naval force into Charleston Harbor, strengthened the garrisons in the forts at that port, and intimated that he was ready to take the field himself to quell an insurrection. He asked Congress for authority to deal with the situation, and for legislation to empower him to enforce the Federal law with the army and navy. But before any blood was shed, Clay introduced his compromise measure for a gradual reduction of duties. Jackson's followers could claim that he had vindicated the supremacy of the Union; Calhoun's followers could assert that he had forced the national government to modify an intolerable tariff law.

This well-drawn cartoon was not the only one that dealt with Nullification. One of the rare newspaper cartoons of the period, in the *United States Weekly Telegraph* of Washington, November 5, 1832, showed the North and South united as Siamese twins; but the South, bending under a heavy burden of "Tariff Taxes," declares: "Union I love to adoration, Death rather than consolidation." An editorial in the same issue defended Nullification—and this in the Nation's capital!

THE DOWNFALL OF MOTHER BANK
BY "ZEK DOWNING." PUBLISHED BY H. R. ROBINSON
[1833]

PRESIDENT JACKSON disliked all banks, particularly Nicholas Biddle's powerful Bank of the United States. When in 1832 Biddle pressed for a renewal of the Bank's charter, he vetoed a bill which Congress passed for the purpose. The Bank, he argued, was undemocratic, unconstitutional, un-American. It was dangerous to concentrate so much power in the hands of a few men "irresponsible to the people." It was time to think of the interest of the masses, and to protect the nation from a dangerous money-power. The doom of the Bank was fixed by the failure to obtain a recharter, and the removal of government funds. It ceased to be a national institution; it had to restrict its operations drastically; in the end it failed. The cartoon shows Jack Downing patting Jackson on the back, wildly applauding his course. Under the crashing pillars are caught Whig politicians and editors, and Biddle himself. The implication that the Bank had supported newspapers, including the Washington *National Intelligencer* and New York *Courier & Enquirer*, with loans and other patronage, was only to well justified.

The cartoonist "Zek Downing" made use of the interest in "Major Jack Downing," a humorous character created by Seba Smith, and the supposed writer of popular letters, in Yankee dialect, on political occurrences.

THE CELESTE-AL CABINET
PUBLISHED BY H. R. ROBINSON
[1834]

JACKSON'S APPOINTMENT of Senator John H. Eaton of Tennessee to be Secretary of War caused a grand social schism in Washington, for Eaton's bride, the former Peggy O'Neill, daughter of an Irish innkeeper, was frowned upon by the more austere ladies of the capital. Mrs. John C. Calhoun, wife of the Vice President, refused to recognize her, as did other prominent women. Jackson, who knew what it was to have his own wife cruelly and unfairly attacked, made his sympathy with Mrs. Eaton entirely plain. This strained social situation contributed to the dramatic breach between Jackson and Calhoun, though other factors (the nullification controversy, and the fact that Calhoun had censured some of Jackson's high-handed acts in Florida) were more important. Celeste was a popular danseuse and actress from Paris, who repeatedly came to the United States, always with success.

OFFICE HUNTERS FOR THE YEAR 1834

PUBLISHED BY ANTHONY IMBERT

[1834]

ANDREW JACKSON'S PART in bringing in the spoils system has been exaggerated, but he unquestionably gave it much greater vigor than it had previously possessed. His predecessors had all but one made partisan appointments. Washington with a few exceptions restricted his choice of officeholders to Federalists, as did John Adams. Jefferson took steps, complaining that "few die and none resign," to replace Federalists with Republicans; before he left the White House he had nearly completed the task. Madison and Monroe maintained a Republican personnel. John Quincy Adams was too conscientious to make removals for party purposes.

Jackson had no such scruples, and ruthlessly displaced hundreds of officeholders in favor of men on whose loyalty he could count. He took the view that appointments had previously gone too largely to men from the upper ranks of life, and that the common man should be given a chance. No great education was required, he said; the duties of public office were so clear and simple "that men of intelligence may readily qualify themselves for their performance." Most of the country sympathized with his belief that natural ability was more important than a college degree. The Jacksonians also pointed out that a great many officials who had hung on from Administration to Administration had become superannuated and inefficient. Besides, good party workers deserved a reward. In New York the Democratic machine or "Albany Regency" had already made lavish use of offices for its supporters. When Van Buren and others helped Jackson carry the system into the national government, W. L. Marcy of New York defended them, saying that he perceived "nothing wrong in the rule that to the victor belong the spoils of the enemy." Hence the phrase "spoils system." Naturally, Clay, J. Q. Adams, and other opponents of the Administration denounced the removals violently. But in the first year and a half of the Jackson regime, they amounted to fewer than a thousand in a total civil service personnel of about ten thousand.

This design, showing Jackson as a winged demon hovering over a crowd of office-seekers, has a faint flavor of the French romantic school of the 1830's. It was possibly inspired by E. LePoitevin's lithographs, "Diableries," which had a great vogue in this period; and perhaps the artist had seen the lithograph of Satan floating in the air which Eugène Delacroix had drawn for Goethe's *Faust*. A good many cartoons of this and later decades dealt with office-hunters. As early as 1836 H. R. Robinson issued a print on the spoils system in New York, showing Van Buren as governor, with a litter of pigs battening at the public trough. Attacks on the system gained special vigor in the days of Cleveland.

SYMPTOMS OF A LOCKED JAW

BY DAVID CLAYPOOLE JOHNSTON
[1834]

THIS SPIRITED CARTOON, which realistically shows Henry Clay sewing up Andrew Jackson's mouth, has more action than was usual in cartoons of that day. It is unusual also in that only two figures tell the story, instead of a whole assemblage of political personages. The diminution in the number of characters makes the point of the drawing much clearer.

Nobody in the late thirties could have missed the point of this picture. Throughout Jackson's eight years in the White House Henry Clay waged a harassing war against him. In this he was abetted by Calhoun, Webster, and a majority of the other Senators. Clay took the view that Jackson's dictatorial ways and inclination to the use of force were a threat to democratic liberties. When the President tried to hasten the destruction of the Bank of the United States by removing the deposits, Clay persuaded the Senate to pass resolutions of censure (1834). Jackson felt outraged. He replied by sending the Senate a formal "protest," which he demanded should be given place in the journal. This protest was a terrific blast against the Senate, an assertion of the place of the President as the "official representative of the American people," and a declaration that if the Senate continued to arraign and censure the conduct of the President, it would "unsettle the foundations of the government." Clay sprang to arms, and had the assistance of Webster and Calhoun. He saw to it that the protest was excluded from the Senate journal; and what was more, he induced the Senate by a vote of 27 to 16, to condemn the protest as an unconstitutional assertion of executive power, and a breach of the privileges of the Senate. Thus he sewed up Jackson's mouth!

Johnston, the versatile etcher, book-illustrator, lithographer, and actor, gained popularity in the thirties by his drawings, which were scattered broadcast by such lithographers as the Pendletons of Boston. The comic annual had become popular in England, where Cruikshank's *Scraps and Sketches* had a wide sale. Johnston caught up the idea, and for a number of years, beginning in 1830, he issued his own etched annual under the title of *Scraps*. Indeed, he was called the American Cruikshank—for his work, original enough in its ideas, showed the influence of the English master. This lithographed cartoon was published separately. The likeness of Clay is remarkably good. The quotation from Hamlet, "Clay might stop a hole, to keep the wind away," is an early example of the literary allusion which later was so frequently used in cartoons.

THE DEBILITATED SITUATION OF A MONARCHAL GOVERNMENT... THE FLOURISHING CONDITION OF A WELL-FORMED INDUSTRIOUS REPUBLIC

ANONYMOUS

[1836]

SOMETHING OF THE SPIRIT of Jefferson Brick animates this cartoon, with its unusual element of a quotation from Byron—a quotation hailing Columbia as the "child and champion" of freedom and as a "Pallas arm'd and undefiled." More than national pride, a bit of boastfulness, goes into the contrast between the strong, prosperous, united America of Andrew Jackson, and the weak, bankrupt, faction-torn France of Louis Philippe. Yet the element of caricature is quite absent; this is a composition in lithography, with a French flavor, rather than a cartoon. Details are carefully carried out, and the figures of Jackson and Louis Philippe are undistorted portraits. But the drawing has but one purpose: to emphasize the superiority of America's republican institutions to those of an effete Old World kingdom.

The cartoon is full of allusions to current events. Jackson reproachfully holds up to the gaze of the French monarch the treaty of July, 1831; that is, the agreement France then signed to pay the United States twenty-five million francs, with some deductions, as compensation for the lawless damages which Napoleon had inflicted upon American shipping. The money was to be turned over in six annual instalments, but the stingy French Chamber refused to make the appropriations. Our lithograph shows the French coffers empty save for a parcel of bills, including charges for a large army and a bloated civil establishment; it shows the American treasury overflowing, as indeed it did, so that on January 1, 1837, large sums of surplus revenue were returned to the States. It shows American citizens eagerly pressing forward to serve the country with their "blood and fortune"; but the French group is a study in indecision and reluctance, while a gendarme has seized a French seaman to hale him back to his ship. In the background we have a warlike confrontation between the American and French navies. This actually took place. The hot-tempered Jackson sent Congress a message denouncing the bad faith of the French, and asking for authority to make reprisals; public feeling in France, already irritated, became angry. The French government broke off diplomatic negotiations with Washington and prepared for hostilities, and for a time a naval conflict seemed almost certain. But finally the French receded, and their Chamber voted the sums required on condition that Jackson withdraw his threats. The blunt-spoken President went so far as to state that he had no desire to insult or injure France, and the spoliation claims were at last paid. The dignity of America had been amply vindicated.

NEW EDITION OF MACBETH.
BANK-OH'S GHOST

BY EDWARD WILLIAMS CLAY

[1837]

A FEW WEEKS AFTER Jackson left the Presidency, the panic of 1837 burst upon the country, and wily Van Buren was forced to deal with a deepening depression. The Whigs naturally regarded the catastrophe as a result of Jackson's war with the Bank of the United States. There was some truth in this view. Jackson had declared in his inaugural address that he doubted whether the Bank (chartered in 1816 by President Monroe) was constitutional, wise in principle, or efficient in creating a sound, uniform currency. The question went into the campaign of 1832. When Jackson was reelected, the Bank was doomed. The government's moneys were deposited in many "pet" banks all over the country, which lent a large part of the funds to speculators in land. Jackson stopped the speculation by the Specie Circular, demanding that all lands above a certain limit be paid for in gold or silver. This created a demand for specie which revealed that most banks held inadequate reserves. Banks began failing, and in May, 1837, they all suspended specie payments. Probably a crash would have come anyhow, but Jackson's ill-informed ideas of public finance first stimulated the land-boom and then helped precipitate the panic.

This cartoon adroitly fastens the blame upon the recent President, the Southern planters, and the rough workingmen of the large cities. We see the "Ghost of Commerce" turning up to haunt them. With pockets full of protested and non-negotiable bills, the ghost lays before Van Buren evidences of general ruin—New York failures of ninety millions; New Orleans failures of seventy millions; Philadelphia failures of forty millions; money six per cent a month. "Repeal the Treasury Order," he demands. Van Buren, as hostile to the Bank as anybody, had been anxious to build up New York as the financial center of the country. He did not lose his nerve, but told an extra session of Congress that he was still against the Bank, and that the people must hew their own way out of "losses by revulsion in commerce and credit." However, it was generally believed that he was sorely frightened, as pictured here. Jackson, stubborn in his alleged errors, is shown as an old termagant with a bowie-knife, ready to shake Van Buren's cowardice out of him. The planter, serenely drinking a julep, is of course against Eastern banks; he does business (theoretically) in specie. The city laborer, labelled "Tammany," is also against banks; he has no money.

Some points of costume are worth noting, especially the planter's high white hat. High hats, from 1830 into the sixties, were an article of dress not only for formal occasions, but for everyday wear.

THE MODERN BALAAM AND HIS ASS

ANONYMOUS

[1837]

THE AUTHOR of this effective cartoon, which evidently appeared just after Jackson gave way to Van Buren, places his emphasis on the Specie Circular. The President's requirement that land offices should cease taking bank notes in payment for public lands, and accept only gold, silver, or land scrip, had struck a heavy blow at public confidence in the banking system. It helped to expose the fact that the banking system of the country possessed a slender store of specie; for when land speculators went to the banks to get some, they were refused. It also proved that the Federal Treasury did not regard the notes of most State banks as sound currency. As the banking system of the country approached disaster, Congress in the last days of the second Jackson Administration passed a bill to annul the Specie Circular. The vote in the Senate was eight to one, in the House nearly three to one. But Jackson gave it a pocket veto, filing his reasons for not signing it. Here he is shown brandishing his veto; the ghostly "bankrupts of 1837" is standing full in his path; in the background are the doors of a long series of banking houses closed by the panic of 1837; and the woebegone Martin Van Buren is beginning to "tread in the footsteps of my illustrious predecessor." This cartoon is well adapted to pin responsibility for the Panic of 1837 upon Jackson. Most surviving cartoons of the period are hostile to Jackson, despite his vast personal popularity. Murrell, in his *American Graphic Humor*, cites a letter (I: 135) written in 1824 by the engraver James Akin to the portrait painter Ralph Earl: "I enclose you a caricature in favor of Gen. Jackson, in opposition to the miserable herd of wretches who publish their pitiful resentments against the Man who saved them from the Grasp of British Tyranny."

A new spirit was now entering American political caricature—a spirit distinctly American. The man most largely responsible for it was H. R. Robinson, lithographic publisher, whose caricature prints show a special character, and an improvement both in composition and in drawing. The presentation in cartoons was rather severely factual. The strong emphasis of caricature, vigorous drawing and effective composition was generally wanting in this period and for some time after. No American artist showed a talent which approached that of Daumier, whose keen wit and vigorous drawing hit the mark so admirably. But Robinson, and later Currier & Ives, issued good work of a factual and rather pedestrian kind.

THE TIMES

BY EDWARD W. CLAY

[1840]

THE TIMES IN 1840 were hard times, for the effects of the panic of '37 still lingered; and graphic realism went into this elaborate cartoon by Clay, with its numerous references to the social life of the day. A run on the Mechanics Bank is going full tilt, with scores trying to crowd into the doorway. Barefoot workmen, despair written on their faces, stand idle in front of a hoarding which advertises a lottery scheme, and money to loan at seven per cent a month. Idle shipping is tied up at the wharf; a manufactory stands grim and silent in the background; and the sheriff is busily auctioning off foreclosed property. The hotel is for sale, and the custom house is doing no business; only the dramshop and the pawnbroker are driving a heavy trade, while across the river the bridewell or prison is receiving a new cartload of inmates. A forlorn widow, garbed in black, with her orphan child beside her, begs alms of a stony-faced Shylock. Over this scene of wretchedness and ruin presides a symbolic emblem, the tall white hat and the silver-bowed spectacles of Andrew Jackson, to all Whigs the author of the general misery. These were the "glory spectacles" said to have been invented by Van Buren. The latter's readiness to present all Jackson's measures as glorious was assumed and satirized in a cartoon of 1833, "Political Firmament as seen through Martin Van Buren's Magic High-Pressure Cabinet Spectacles."

This well-balanced lithograph, produced for the log-cabin campaign of this year, must have had an instant appeal to all who felt that the times were out of joint; whether they had lost their money in the banks operated on the safety-fund principle, were out of work, or had to lament the fact that flour fetched fourteen dollars a barrel. The print, with its swarming figures and vigorous action, its effective composition, its variety, though not a notable production of art, stands in contrast to the generality of contemporary cartoons, with their stiff alignment of figures. For while here also there is multiplicity of detail crowded into the picture in the attempt to give a complete cross-section of the period's conditions and problems, at least there is a certain vivacity in treatment that helps to stress the point to be made. On the hoarding above referred to the publisher slips in an advertisement for his wares: "Caricatures 52 Courtlandt St. H. R. Robinson."

CLAR DE KITCHEN

ISSUED BY H. R. ROBINSON; SIGNED "BONEYSHANKS"

[1840]

CONSTANCE ROURKE tells us in *Roots of American Culture* that "Clar de Kitchen" was one of the favorite dance songs of T. D. Rice, the popularizer of Jim Crow and leader in Negro minstrelsy. No doubt this title refers to the song. William Henry Harrison, as an enraged housewife, is about to clear the kitchen of Matty Van Buren and his associates and followers. The whole Democratic leadership is being ejected. Calhoun breaks for the door, declaring "I am for the South direct." Levi Woodbury, the Secretary of the Treasury, is in consternation; "I can issue no more Treasury Notes!" he laments. "I shall never be Vice President," says William Smith of Alabama, who had aspired to that position. Joel R. Poinsett, the Secretary of of War, remarks that if Van Buren had followed his advice, "we would have had by this time our Standing Army of 200,000 men." The lean and nervous Francis P. Blair, who as party editor had served Jackson and Van Buren so ably, is particularly disgusted, and strides across a fallen chair with the words, "I will leave the *Globe!*" Others of note appear. But the saddest figure is Van Buren. "This is worse than the rebellion in Vermont!" he declares—for while he had carried Maine, New Hampshire, Rhode Island, and Connecticut, Harrison had swept Vermont by a vote of approximately 21,000 to 14,000.

Van Buren naturally came in for his share of the attacks made on Jackson and his followers, as appears from several cartoons reproduced in the present volume. The nicknames "Fox" and "The Little Magician," applied to him, were used to good effect by cartoonists, for example in "Old Jack in the last Agony" (1837) and "The Little Magician invoked" (1844).

The identity of "Boneyshanks" (a signature probably suggested by Cruikshank's name) is unknown; lithographing houses like that of H. R. Robinson now had a number of artists to choose from, and many of the best cartoons were anonymous. This drawing has vitality and energy, and the number of rather careful portraits in the group give it unusual historical interest.

POLITICAL CLIMBING BOYS

ANONYMOUS

[1844]

BAD AS POLITICAL PROPHECY, this is a good campaign cartoon, well calculated to hearten Whigs and to persuade Democrats that their candidate was doing badly. The year 1844 found the question of the annexation of Texas uppermost in the public mind. The Whigs, unanimously nominating Henry Clay, made no allusion to Texas in their platform. The Democrats held a hectic convention, in which after much balloting the dark horse James K. Polk emerged as victor. It was well known that he advocated the acquisition of Texas, and the platform called both for the taking of the whole of Oregon, and for "reannexation" of the Texan Republic. Meanwhile, Tyler in the White House and Calhoun in the Senate were pressing for immediate action. When the Senate rejected a treaty for the acquisition of Texas, it was brought into the Union by joint resolution of Congress—before Tyler left the Presidency.

Midway in the campaign this cartoon would have seemed justified by the facts. The Whigs were enthusiastically behind Clay. Polk was little known, and his candidacy seemed artificial. Thomas Hart Benton is here portrayed assisting him with his mop—the mop that had expunged the Senate resolution of censure against Jackson from the journal; Jackson is lending a hand, and Calhoun cheering the candidate on. Beyond question, Clay was the most popular man in the country. But his popularity did not avail him. The Democrats were determined to have Texas; the Whigs were divided on that issue. When Clay took an equivocal stand, the little body of Abolitionist or Liberty Party voters went for a candidate of their own. Polk won by the narrowest of margins in the popular vote—a majority of about 38,000 over Clay. Had the Abolitionists cast their ballots for Clay instead of James G. Birney, the Kentuckian would have had a popular majority of about 30,000, and a majority of seven in the electoral college.

A cartoon, "The Great American Steeplechase for 1844," by E. W. Clay, presents the Whig candidate riding an animal half-alligator, half-horse, and boasting: "Hurrah! Old Kentuck will distance them yet." But it lacks the graphic merit of this drawing, in which the figures of Benton, Jackson, and Calhoun are especially well rendered, and in which Van Buren, Tyler, Webster and Scott also appear. Clay's prominence in public affairs made him a target for the shafts of the cartoonists. His attitude on the tariff question is dealt with in "Old Harry Senior and Old Harry Junior" and "Whig Appeal for an Excuse." And in "The Man wot drives the Constitution" (1844) Clay, Frelinghuysen, and others appear on "Salt River," a locality figuring fairly frequently in later cartoons.

ALL THE MORALITY AND ALL THE RELIGION
ANONYMOUS
[1844]

THIS AMUSING CARTOON is based upon the contrast between the private lives of the two Whig candidates in 1844, Henry Clay and Theodore Frelinghuysen. Frelinghuysen, well known as a lawyer and a Senator from New Jersey, had a national reputation for rigidity of morals and depth of religious conviction. He was dubbed "the Christian statesman"; ministers often extolled him from the pulpit; and William Lloyd Garrison addressed a poem to him because of his defense of the much-abused Cherokee Indians, hailing him as "Patriot and Christian." He felt a deep solicitude over the religious beliefs of his associates in politics, and was bold enough to exhort Webster, Clay, and other leaders to make themselves right with God. At one time he thought of leaving politics, and entering the ministry. On the other hand, Henry Clay enjoyed all the good things of life. He liked to attend horse-races and cockfighting matches; he drank in moderation—much more moderately than Webster—and he was adept at cards. John Quincy Adams and Clay were commissioners to the Peace Conference at Ghent in 1815. Adams records in his diary that more than once, when he rose at five o'clock to begin the day's work, he heard a convivial card party in Clay's rooms across the entry just breaking up. Nor did Clay draw the line at duelling. His famous exchange of shots with John Randolph of Roanoke in 1826, which ended in a friendly handshake, was called by Thomas Hart Benton "about the last high-toned duel that I have witnessed."

In the cartoon Clay is explaining to the credulous Frelinghuysen that the sporting prints on the wall, and the playing-cards on the shelf, all have a Biblical significance, or are at any rate quite harmless. He and Randolph merely shot at a mark one day. It was a favorite vaunt of the Whigs that their party represented more decorum and principle than did the rowdy Democrats, so strong on the frontier and in the slums, and so weak in the polished circles of aristocratic society. While the attitude of Clay and Frelinghuysen is stiffly histrionic, and the long speeches in the loops are awkward, the public doubtless found the cartoon a palpable hit. One somewhat like it, also brought out in 1844, was entitled "Virtuous Harray, or Set a Thief to Catch a Thief." It showed Polk welcoming Texas to the "land of the brave," while Clay addressed her threateningly: "Stand back, Madam Texas. . . . Do you think we will have anything to do with gamblers, horse-racers, and licentious profligates?" A Quaker standing by remarks: "Softly . . . Thou hast mentioned the very reason that we cannot vote for thee."

FUNERAL OBSEQUIES OF FREE-TRADE

BY EDWARD W. CLAY

[1846]

TARIFF BARRIERS in the forties seemed to be going down the world over. In England Richard Cobden and John Bright had taken the leadership in a crusade against the Corn Laws or tariffs on food. "I be protected and I be starving," was the farm laborer's speech that they quoted. The Irish famine of 1846 lent impetus to the movement. In that year the Corn Laws went overboard; Great Britain abandoned protectionist doctrines in favor of the views of the apostles of *laissez-faire*; cheap food and cheap raw materials gave new energy to manufacturing. The year 1848, when the Continent was aflame with revolution, found England prosperous and wages rising. In the United States, Polk's Secretary of the Treasury, Robert J. Walker, held the general doctrines of the *laissez-faire* leaders in Britain. In 1846 he was the principal architect of a new tariff which, strongly supported by the South and West, became law in midsummer. It was not a free trade law, but a moderate protectionist measure—hence this cartoon. But compared with later American tariffs, it was extremely low. The country prospered under it, and manufacturing grew. The cartoonist indicates the fact that the measure represented a compromise, and did not go so far as some Democratic leaders—Polk, Buchanan, Marcy, and Dallas—were supposed to wish. The sheet marked "50 cents" in Marcy's pocket is a reference to the current story that while governor of New York, he had sent in a bill for travelling expenses which included "for patching trousers, 50¢."

THE GOOD BOY WHO GAVE AWAY HIS CAKE

FROM "YANKEE DOODLE"

[1846]

WEAK AS A DRAWING, this cartoon—showing Victoria, Prince of Wales, and Master Yankee Doodle—touches on an important subject; the fact that since the repeal of the Corn Laws, the United States had become the great supplier of grain for the British workers. By the time of the Civil War, Northern wheat was to be quite as important to England as Southern cotton. The tone of the cartoon brings out the fact that low tariffs are a potent source of good will, as high tariffs are potent breeders of animosity.

MEDIATION AND PACIFICATION

BY EDWARD W. CLAY

[1846]

WHEN THIS CARTOON APPEARED, the Mexican War was well under way and American victory certain. General Taylor had invaded Mexico, taking Matamoras and Monterey; General Kearny had advanced into New Mexico, capturing Santa Fé without a battle; and following the "Bear Flag Revolution," Commodore Sloat had hoisted the American flag in California and proclaimed its annexation. All this was watched jealously by the European Powers. Great Britain had hoped that Texas, to which considerable numbers of Britons had emigrated, would maintain her independence. Though the British Government had never been actively interested in obtaining California, some British agents had been busy there, and most Americans suspected Downing Street of secret designs to keep the province out of American hands.

Here we have a compact summary of the political and diplomatic situation as Easterners saw it in the autumn of 1846. President Polk had concluded that the offer of a large sum in cash might persuade the Paredes Government in Mexico to conclude a satisfactory treaty. He asked Congress for two millions "to facilitate negotiations," and such prominent Whigs as Daniel Webster and Tom Corwin supported the request. The cartoonist supports it too; he shows the great cannon "Peacemaker" delivering the two millions "Secret Service Money" to Paredes, while in the background Mexican and American armies (represented by two fighting cocks) face each other belligerently. Robert J. Walker, Secretary of the Treasury and chief author of the Walker Tariff which went into effect this year, is delivering additional money-bags to Polk. Congress, as a matter of fact, adjourned without taking action on the bill to appropriate two millions. It was not money that was delivered to Mexico early in 1847, but the invading troops of Winfield Scott's army.

The supposed concern of Louis Philippe and Queen Victoria in an early peace is rather mildly portrayed. The queen never offered her services as mediator, and the British actually cared little when California came under the American flag. Public opinion in England was in fact greatly impressed by the prowess of the American troops. All the likenesses in the picture do credit to Edward W. Clay's skill as a draughtsman. It is to be noted that the far horizon shows the American flag floating over Santa Fé and Monterey.

This golden discharge is more to my taste than the laurels I should reap on the banks of the Sabine.

Guizot tells me these Yankees must be looked after, or they'll take the whole of Mexico. I shall send a fleet of observation to the Gulf at once.

Friend Polk, let me offer my services as mediator. I just know I've an interest in the matter whatever it may be. I want you to get California!

Friend Victoria, I respectfully decline your offer, whenever just put your finger in the pie, you are sure to make a mess of it, we can manage our own affairs well enough, without the interference of foreign powers! We'll ever give me some more ammunition.

PEACE MAKER

U.S.A.

THE MEXICAN COMMANDER ENJOYING THE PROSPECT OPPOSITE MATAMORAS

LITHOGRAPH BY SARONY & MAJOR. PUBLISHED BY THOMAS W. STRONG

[1846]

May in 1846 brought war with Mexico—a war that had really been inevitable ever since the annexation of Texas the previous year. The Mexican leaders were eager for a conflict, and felt certain that they could win against the cowardly Yankees. Polk would gladly have paid twenty or twenty-five millions for New Mexico and California, but the mission he sent down to Mexico City to arrange a peaceful settlement failed. When fighting began, the country went into the conflict with unexpected enthusiasm. It was full of contempt for the Mexicans; and the few cartoons that the war produced were nearly all of a spreadeagle, Jefferson Brick type, full of brag and jingoism. The first action of the American troops had been to advance to the Rio Grande opposite Matamoras. In this fine caricature, General Santa Anna is shown staring with angry astonishment at the forces under Zachary Taylor. "These Northern barbarians!" he exclaims. "Where is my friend John Bull?" The ambling nag, the spindle-bodied President, the grotesque head, the protruding eyes—these all have a fine comic effect. The drawing shows the style of Napoleon Sarony, and has a freedom not common at the time.

UNCLE SAM'S TAYLORIFICS

BY EDWARD W. CLAY

[1846]

American boastfulness could not be better expressed than in this picture of Brother Jonathan striding across the Rio Grande to cut Mexico in two with a huge scissors, one blade of which is labelled Gen. Taylor (that is, the regular army), and the other the Volunteers. "You come to steal my new boot?" he ejaculates—the new boot being Texas. "I'll discumgalligumfriate you!" A sly-looking John Bull is fishing for Oregon with a hook marked 49 degrees, but is patently willing to take the 54° 40′ line if he cannot do better. In these days when Americans prepared to march to "the halls of the Montezumas," talked of "Fifty-four forty or fight," and believed themselves the beneficiaries of "manifest destiny," they thought their posturing heroic when it was actually rather comic in its self-complacency and rather irritating in its bluster.

JOSHUA COMMANDING THE SUN TO STAND STILL

BY W. F. C.
[1848]

"Let us show at least as much spirit in defending our rights and honor as they [the non-slaveholding States] have evinced in assailing them. . . . Henceforward, let all party distinctions among us cease, so long as this aggression on our rights and honor shall continue." So Calhoun exhorted a great Charleston audience on March 8, 1847, some six months after Representative David Wilmot of Pennsylvania had offered in Congress his famous Proviso excluding slavery from all the Territories to be acquired from Mexico. The Proviso did not pass Congress, but it was the signal that the slavery controversy had entered upon a new and more dangerous phase. The crisis had begun which made necessary, within the next three years after Calhoun's speech, the formulation of the Compromise of 1850, a compromise which healed the sectional controversy but imperfectly and only for a short time.

This cartoon, boldly holding Calhoun up to condemnation, is among the many tokens of the critical new phase in the slavery struggle. It exposes one of the chief weaknesses of the Southern position. South Carolina and other slave States had long since refused to permit any discussion of the merits of slavery within their borders. They declined to permit anti-slavery publications to circulate. Even on free soil sympathizers with slavery had attacked the offices of Abolitionist journals. Elijah Lovejoy was murdered at Alton when he persisted in publishing his paper; J. G. Birney could not issue his anti-slavery publication in Cincinnati save at the risk of his life. Throughout the South freedom of assemblage, freedom of speech, and freedom of the press were rigidly restricted. The right of petition, the free use of the mails, and in some instances the right of jury trial, were denied. These invasions of fundamental Anglo-Saxon liberties, with repeated instances of mob violence, converted many fair-minded Northerners to an anti-slavery position. Salmon P. Chase of Ohio, for example, took up the cause after he witnessed infringements upon the freedom of the press in southern Ohio; Gerrit Smith after he saw a mob break up an anti-slavery meeting at Utica. White rights as well as black rights, said these men, were in question.

The artist, whose identity is unknown, achieves his effect with great economy. A single figure, graphically presented, a single speech—and he has driven his point home. Here, as in many of the mid-century cartoons, we have quite good portraiture, without caricature.

"Sun of Intellectual light & liberty, stand ye still, in Masterly inactivity, that the Nation of Carolina may continue to hold Negroes & plant Cotton till the day of Judgment!"

SLAVERY IN AMERICA ... IN ENGLAND
ANONYMOUS. PUBLISHED BY J. HAVEN, BOSTON
[1850]

NOTHING DELIGHTED Southern apologists more than to contrast the happy existence of the carefree, kindly treated Negro and the harsh lot of the wage-slave in a Yankee or British factory. When Mrs. Stowe published *Uncle Tom's Cabin*, Mrs. Mary H. Eastman promptly answered her in *Aunt Phillie's Cabin, or, Southern Life as it is*. One of the characters, a Virginian, rebukes an Englishman who invites him to come to the mother country, land of universal emancipation. "The old State is good enough for me," he says. "I have been to England, and I saw some of your redeemed, regenerated, disenthralled people; I saw features on women's faces that haunted me afterwards in my dreams. I saw children with shrivelled, attenuated limbs, and countenances that were old in misery and vice."

The cartoon presents exuberantly healthy Negroes, well dressed, footing a hoe-down to music. Two Northern visitors listen as Southern planters tell them that the Negroes are free after four or five in the afternoon to enjoy themselves. But Southern historians such as Charles S. Sydnor have assured us that hours of work were seldom so easy. Similarly, the cartoon gives an overdrawn picture of British "slavery." Order is kept at a "cloth factory" by soldiers; a fat priest and a tax-gatherer gaze contemptuously on stunted, emaciated, ragged factory hands who bemoan their hard lot. One lad asserts his intention of running away from the mill, where he works seventeen hours a day, to a coal-mine where he will toil only fourteen. Actually Parliament had in 1819 limited the working day of youths below sixteen to twelve hours. In 1847 it fixed a ten-hour day for women and youths in textile factories, and since grown men could seldom carry on operations alone, this practically prescribed a ten-hour day for the industry. The cartoon would have been more truthful, though less effective, had it been more moderate in its claims for chattel slavery and its indictment of industrialism alike.

From the prominence it gives to George Thompson, the English anti-slavery crusader, it appears that this cartoon was evoked by his second visit to the United States in 1850. In 1834–35 he came to this country on the invitation of William Lloyd Garrison and made a lecture tour so brilliantly successful that he barely escaped with his life. Mobs attacked him and his audience and drove him out of Boston to Canada. On his return tour in 1850–51 he again encountered much hostility. But he made a triumphant journey through New England and upper New York, speaking to large audiences, and was given a banquet in Boston. The cartoon had a Boston publisher. It doubtless pleased the many "solid" men of that city who disliked to see the slavery question agitated.

SLAVERY AS IT EXISTS IN AMERICA.

SLAVERY AS IT EXISTS IN ENGLAND.

THOMPSON,
THE ENGLISH ANTI SLAVERY AGITATOR.

PRACTICAL ILLUSTRATION OF THE FUGITIVE SLAVE LAW

BY E. C.
[1851]

THIS LITHOGRAPH epitomizes the feeling of anti-slavery men upon the Fugitive Slave Act passed in 1850 as part of the great Compromise. The law was severe. It permitted owners pursuing an alleged fugitive to seize him without process of law; it laid heavy penalties upon anybody who assisted a fugitive to escape; it required all good citizens to assist in the execution of the law; and it debarred the alleged fugitive from giving testimony when the case came to trial. Thousands of Negroes who had been settled in the North for years, found reputable employment, built homes, and reared families, were now in danger of being dragged back into servitude. It was not difficult to kidnap a free Negro on the pretext that he was a slave. It at once became evident that the new law was certain to produce serious friction. Many Northerners, including prominent ministers, openly defied it. The newspapers were soon full of news of rescues or attempted rescues of fugitive blacks, while some of the most noted statesmen of the North went into the law courts to defend alleged fugitives. Salmon P. Chase of Ohio, for example, was soon called "attorney general for runaway Negroes." The Underground Railroad pursued its work of transporting fugitives across the free States into Canada more zealously than ever. Before long, moreover, numerous States of the North were placing "personal liberty laws" on their statute books to nullify the Federal enactment—laws which gave legal protection to Negroes under pursuit. There could be no question that, despite clear constitutional guarantees, most of the North was averse to seeing slave owners recapture their property when it took to flight and crossed the Mason and Dixon Line or the Ohio River. The publication of *Uncle Tom's Cabin* intensified this feeling.

This cartoon, a bit freer in drawing than cartoons generally at that time, appeals to Northern indignation over the law, showing an arrogant slaveholder riding the bitted Daniel Webster, a rope and a fetter in his hand, while Garrison defends a cowering black woman. In another cartoon, "No Higher Law," Webster holds a scroll inscribed "I propose to support that bill to the fullest extent." E. W. Clay's "What's Sauce for the Goose is Sauce for the Gander" argues that the game of detaining property is one that two can play. The benevolent Northern merchant refuses to give up to the Southern planter his runaway servant; the Southerner turns the tables by declining to give up to the merchant the goods that he has shipped down South. Both appeal to what W. H. Seward had called "the higher law."

OSTEND DOCTRINE: PRACTICAL DEMOCRATS CARRYING OUT THE PRINCIPLE

BY LOUIS MAURER
[1854]

No sooner had the Mexican War closed than American expansionists turned their eyes toward Cuba. The prize particularly appealed to those Southerners who regarded the admission of California as a free State, under the Compromise of 1850, as unfair; they held that the South was entitled to Cuba as compensation. In the spring of 1852 the British Government proposed that the United States, Britain, and France enter into a tripartite agreement not to permit any nation to acquire Cuba from Spain. The American Secretary of State, Edward Everett, refused in a vigorous dispatch. In a drawing, "The Eagle and the Wren," published in *The Lantern* in 1852, Thomas Butler Gunn depicts the United States (a cross between Uncle Sam and an eagle) watching with elation as the Cuban wren flies away from Queen Isabella of Spain; the Spanish lion astounded and angry. The cartoon summed up the hopes of a great part of the American people.

The fever for Cuban annexation reached its climax in 1854. President Pierce, spurred on by Southern expansionists and by such Northerners as the banker August Belmont, was eager to make his Administration memorable by acquiring the island. He sent instructions to American representatives in Europe which brought about a meeting of the ministers to Britain, Spain, and France at Ostend to enunciate a Cuban policy. With James Buchanan as the leading spirit, they issued the celebrated Ostend Manifesto. This asserted that the United States could never rest content until it possessed Cuba, that Spain ought to sell it, and that, if a fair offer of purchase were refused and Spanish tenure became endangered, "then, by every law, human and divine, we shall be justified in wresting it from Spain if we possess the power." This was the doctrine of highwaymen, and Secretary of State Marcy repudiated it. The manifesto caused great indignation both in Europe and the United States. Maurer was one of the ablest artists employed by Currier and Ives; his cartoons, in drawing and facial expression, stand out from most of the work at that time. In the present one four thugs are explaining to the dismayed Buchanan that "considerations exist" which render it of "paramount importance" that he hand over his wallet, watch and hat immediately.

"If ye don't hand over yer small change in a jiffy, ye auld spal- peen, I'll feel justified in taking it out of ye wid a touch of this shillaly as I praises the power."

"Come lets have that ticker or you'll find that 'Conside- rations exist which render delay' in doing so 'Exce- dingly dangerous to your head.'"

"Off with this Coat old fellow 'and be quick about it or it's not improbable' that it may be 'wrested from you' by a success- ful revolution of this six barreled joker."

"Why! Why! this is rank robbery! Help! Help! all honest men!"

"I'll take yer hat Old Buck, I havn't got none and as I may catch a cold in my head its 'immediate acquisi- tion' by me 'is of paramount importance.'"

OSTEND MANIFESTO
October 18th 1854.—

The Union can never enjoy repose nor possess reliable security as long as Cuba is not embraced with- in its boundaries. Its acquisition is of paramount importance by our Government. Considera- tions exist which render delay in the acquisition of this Island exceedingly dangerous to the United States. That it is not improbable therefore that Cuba may be wrested from Spain by a successful Revolution. We shall be justified in wresting it from Spain if we possess the Power.

Yours respectfully

JAMES BUCHANAN.
J. Y. MASON.
PIERRE SOULE.
Hon. W. L. MARCY,
Secretary of State.

FANCIED SECURITY, OR THE RATS ON A BENDER

BY LOUIS MAURER

[1856]

MILLARD FILLMORE, as an honest old farmer with a club, watches the predatory antics of the rats James Buchanan, John C. Frémont, and others, anxious to lay their paws on offices and contracts. This was the kind of cartoon that Americans or Know-Nothings, with a surviving band of Whigs, hung in their shop-windows as the three-cornered campaign of 1856 grew hotter. Buchanan tells John C. Breckinridge, his Southern running-mate, that if he hadn't lost his Democratic blood when young he might win—for Buchanan began life as a Federalist. Frémont clambers in sight of the fodder, William C. Dayton, Republican nominee for Vice President, hanging onto his tail. Two well-known editors cheer Frémont on. Greeley, always the reformer and idealist, wants just one squeak more for freedom, while James Gordon Bennett is quite sure that the coast is clear. This cartoon makes the most of Fillmore's well-established reputation for honesty, Buchanan's reputation for feebleness of will, and the general suspicion that the Republicans who professed to be so austerely virtuous really had a shrewd eye on pelf and power.

For an excited and angry campaign, fought in an atmosphere thick with charges and counter-charges over slavery, the Brooks-Sumner affair, and "bleeding Kansas," this is a remarkably good-natured caricature. Many a friendship was broken in that summer of 1856. Threats of Southern secession if Frémont were elected became more numerous and earnest. For a time it looked as if bloodshed were a possibility. But the Democrats actually had little trouble in winning. For one reason, the Republican Party was too new to be strongly organized or well supported financially. For another, the talk of secession caused tens of thousands of conservative men to vote for Buchanan and against the "sectional" candidacy of Frémont. In the October elections Pennsylvania went Democratic. The final result was a foregone conclusion. Buchanan gained 174 electoral votes; Frémont, carrying eleven States, had only 114; while Fillmore won only Maryland, with 8 votes.

Never had a campaign inspired so much activity among caricaturists as this one. Currier & Ives cheerfully furnished pictures for all parties, while other lithographers were busy. A "buck hunt," "Buck taking the pot" in a poker game, a sweepstakes race—in which one of the horses is "Old Buck by Filibuster out of Federalist"—these were among the devices used. One of the wittiest prints, "A Serviceable Garment," recalled Buchanan's part in issuing the Ostend Manifesto. Holding up an old coat, he ejaculates "That Cuba patch to be sure is rather unsightly, but it suits Southern fashions at this season."

THE GREAT REPUBLICAN REFORM PARTY CALLING ON THEIR CANDIDATE

BY LOUIS MAURER

[1856]

THE REPUBLICAN PARTY, which named that glamorous explorer Frémont as its first candidate for President, was the outgrowth of a great moral uprising produced by the Kansas-Nebraska Act, the attempted enforcement of the Fugitive Slave Law, and other so-called aggressions of slavery. Its fervent enthusiasm, strong idealistic tinge, and attraction for all radical-minded Northerners made it easy for opponents to attack it as a party of long-haired men and short-haired women, of eccentrics, cranks and windbags. For several years the temperance movement had been a force in politics; Maine had passed her famous prohibitory law in 1851, and it was widely copied in the North. In Massachusetts, New York, Michigan and other States nearly all important advocates of a Maine law were anti-slavery men. The Women's Rights movement was in full swing; not yet primarily a crusade for the ballot, but rather a demand for equality in marriage, education, property-holding, and employment. Its leaders—Wendell Phillips, Lucy Stone, William Lloyd Garrison, Lucretia Mott, Elizabeth Cady Stanton— were also hostile to slavery. (Most Americans still held that woman's place was the home, and showered the "mental Amazons" with ridicule.) The labor movement was growing stronger, and demanding a ten-hour day and other reforms. Its sympathizers too were likely to be Abolitionists or free-soilers. William Lloyd Garrison held smoking in abhorrence, while Horace Greeley was a conspicuous advocate of vegetarianism and other isms. All this made it easy to identify Republicanism with all kinds of dubious or sinister vagaries.

Maurer's lithograph, issued by Currier & Ives, makes the most of the idea that Frémont was supported by a motley and disreputable crew. An overdressed Negro, demanding equality of the colored population; a delightfully mature spinster who advocates free love; a ruffianly laborer with whiskey-bottle in hand insisting on a general division of property; a feminist dressed in Amelia Bloomer's costume and smoking a cigar to show that she uses all the male prerogatives; a lanky, hard-jawed puritanical reformer who is going to do away with tobacco, meat, and beer—these are the Republican Party. A prominent place is taken by a priest, for it was one of the Democratic fictions of the campaign that Frémont (actually an Episcopalian) was a Catholic. The cartoon is absurdly unfair, but has a certain wit. It is to be noted that although Frémont enjoyed great personal popularity, cartoonists for the most part dealt adversely with him. So, in "Col. Fremont's last Grand Exploring Expedition" (Currier & Ives) he is on "Abolition Nag," pulled by Seward toward "Salt River."

is a law making the use of Tobacco, Animal food and Lager bier a Capital Crime—

of all; the recognition of Woman as the equal of man with a right to vote and hold office—

sion of Property that is what I go in for—

next meeting of our Free Love association, where the shackles of marriage are not tolerated & perfect Freedom exist in love matters and you will be sure to Enjoy yourself, for we are all Freemasons—

you Sir to place the power of the Pope on a firm footing in this country.

ob Color comes in first — arter dat, you may do wot you pleases—

and be sure that the glorious Principles of Popery, Fourierism, Free Love, Woman's rights, the Maine Law, & above all the Equality of our Colored brethren, shall be maintained. If I get into the Presidential chair.

LIBERTY, THE FAIR MAID OF KANSAS—
IN THE HANDS OF "BORDER RUFFIANS"

ANONYMOUS
[1856]

IF THE DEBATE over the Kansas-Nebraska Bill created intense bitterness, the course of events in Kansas rapidly deepened it. The Territory was no sooner opened to settlement than the North and South became competitors to see which would populate and hold it. Eli Thayer formed his Emigrant Aid Society, and similar Northern organizations sprang into existence to help free-soil settlers establish homes. The pro-slavery men of Missouri, armed to the teeth, poured across the boundary whenever an election was held to control it by force and fraud. By the spring of 1856 civil war was raging in Kansas. Slavery men, holding the Missouri River approaches, attacked parties of Northerners. When a free-state government was set up in Lawrence, a pro-slavery mob seized the town, smashed the newspaper offices, fired numerous buildings, and retired with a burden of loot. On the heels of this outrage John Brown of Osawatomie, to avenge the murder of various freesoilers, coolly murdered five adherents of slavery. The result was general lawlessness and widespread fighting. News of all this aroused intense feeling—particularly in the North, where press and pulpit harped upon the alleged attempt to make Kansas a slave State by violence.

The point of this cartoon is the jovial acquiescence of the Democratic leaders in Kansas maraudings and murders. The background presents harrowing incidents supposed to be daily occurring in Kansas: an emigrant train under attack, defenseless men being clubbed and stabbed, a woman being shot down, another gone mad under her sufferings. In the foreground the principal Democratic chieftains—President Pierce, Secretary of State Marcy, Candidate Buchanan, and the two men most closely identified with squatter-sovereignty doctrine, Cass and Douglas—are revelling in license and disorder. The implication is that as they were responsible for the measures leading to these Kansas crimes, and were doing nothing to stop the lawlessness, they were accomplices in the crimes themselves. Pierce had shown timidity and weakness in dealing with the Kansas question; his appointment of the pro-slavery Wilson Shannon as governor had been unpardonable. When Buchanan became President, he was to be even more pusillanimous and blundering.

It is a savage cartoon, but not more savage than Charles Sumner's famous speech of this year upon "The Crime against Kansas." It overstated the case against Pierce and his associates. But it was part of the effective propaganda which in 1854–56 caused many previously moderate Northerners to face the slavery issue with new determination. The ostrich attitude of ignoring the painful slavery question was beginning to disappear, and the sectional issue was often treated with blunt directness.

SOUTHERN CHIVALRY—ARGUMENT VERSUS CLUB'S

BY J. L. MAGEE

[1856]

Sumner's speech on "The Crime against Kansas," delivered in the Senate on May 19–20, 1856, had a dramatic and shocking sequel. His treatment of the Kansas difficulties was bad enough in its exaggerations and partisanship. But much worse was his attack upon the State of South Carolina as a blot upon civilization, and his personal abuse of an absent South Carolina Senator, Andrew Pickens Butler. Sumner's outburst aroused general indignation. Cass of Michigan characterized it as "unpatriotic" and "un-American" in the highest degree. It might well have been left to condemn itself. But one of Senator Butler's kinsmen, Representative Preston S. Brooks, unfortunately felt that considerations of personal honor required him to inflict chastisement upon Sumner. Entering the Senate chamber after adjournment, when it was nearly empty, he approached Sumner, who was busily writing at his desk, accosted him, and struck him repeatedly over the head with a heavy gutta-percha cane. The Massachusetts Senator fell to the floor bleeding and unconscious. He required three years to recover—during which time angry Massachusetts kept his seat vacant for him.

Northern resentment over this incident was intense, and freesoil cartoonists and editors made the most of it. "Violence reigns in the streets of Washington," wrote William Cullen Bryant; "violence has now found its way into the Senate chamber. Violence lies in wait on all the navigable rivers and all the railways of Missouri, to obstruct those who pass from the free States into Kansas. Violence overhangs the frontiers of that Territory like a stormcloud charged with hail and lightning. . . . In short, violence is the order of the day; the North is to be pushed to the wall by it, and this plot will succeed if the people of the free States are as apathetic as the slaveholders are insolent." One of the most striking incidents of the decade, the Brooks-Sumner affair fired the hearts of millions of Northerners, while in the South Brooks was widely applauded for his "spirited" course. The event left the two sections farther apart than ever. Incidentally, it strengthened the Republican Party, and it gave Sumner new prestige as a martyr to a great cause. The assailant was shown in another cartoon, "Right Man in Right Place," as "Bully Brooks" in the stocks, being pelted with vegetables and dead cats and dogs.

In the present cartoon, the two figures fill up most of the space, and there is a solidity, a sweep in the drawing which the caricaturists of the day rarely showed.

THE LITTLE GIANT—IN THE CHARACTER OF THE GLADIATOR

ANONYMOUS

[1858]

No EVENT OF THE FIFTIES was more dramatic than Douglas's break with the Buchanan Administration when the President urged Congress to admit Kansas into the Union under the pro-slavery Lecompton Constitution. That Constitution was regarded by the vast majority of Northerners as a fraud and a swindle. The free-state men in Kansas had refused to participate in the convention which drew it up, and had in general abstained from voting on it when it was submitted. But President Buchanan took the view that the constitution was valid, and declared that "Kansas is . . . at this moment as much a slave State as Georgia or South Carolina." Douglas, who felt in honor bound to see that his doctrine of popular sovereignty was fairly applied, showed great courage in opposing the Administration, which had the solid weight of most of the South behind it. He was immediately read out of the party by all its regular leaders. When the bill for admission came before the Senate, he took his stand with men whom for years he had been attacking—with Sumner, Wade, Seward, and other Republicans. No part of his public career was more creditable than this. In the end, Buchanan was decisively beaten on the issue. Though the bill for admitting Kansas passed the Senate, it was known that it could not possibly get through the House. A compromise bill was therefore presented—the "English Bill"—under which the Lecompton Constitution was to be resubmitted to the voters of Kansas. When this resubmission took place, the Constitution was rejected by an overwhelming vote.

It is to be noted that in this cartoon, as in that entitled "Liberty, the Fair Maid of Kansas," Douglas is shown with full chin-beard and shaven upper lip. His use of the beard was brief; no known portrait shows him with it. It is also to be noted that in the background Robert J. Walker is struggling with Buchanan over the Kansas issue. Walker, whom we have met before as Polk's Secretary of the Treasury, had shown great firmness, as governor of Kansas Territory, in maintaining the rights of the settlers and throwing out fraudulent election returns. He opposed Buchanan's Lecompton policy, and in 1857 resigned with a letter in which he attacked the President and his course, and gave powerful support to Douglas. While Walker fights with Buchanan, the background shows the power of the free press trampling down the prostrate figure of the Washington *Globe*, the Administration organ. Altogether, this was a cartoon for the Douglas Democrats, the voters who accepted his slogan, "Let the Voice of the People Rule."

"WELL! LET EM COME ON, WE'RE ARM'D."

THE GREAT MATCH AT BALTIMORE, BETWEEN THE "ILLINOIS" BANTAM AND THE "OLD COCK" OF THE WHITE HOUSE

ANONYMOUS. PUBLISHED BY CURRIER & IVES

[1860]

DEMOCRATIC DISSENSION IN 1860 and the complete downfall of Buchanan are the themes of this effective cartoon. The interest of every American was focussed on the coming Presidential contest. The Democratic Party was split between an extreme Southern wing demanding Federal laws to protect slavery in the Territories, and the Douglas wing, which demanded that the Territories be allowed to deal with slavery for themselves. Buchanan was of course aligned with the extremists. Could the party hold together? When the Convention met in Charleston, Douglas had a majority of the delegates and had the platform written as he desired; but he did not have the two-thirds majority required to gain the nomination. When the platform was adopted without reference to a slave code, four Southern States, led by South Carolina and Alabama, withdrew, and most delegates from four other States followed. The convention adjourned to meet in Baltimore. Again the Douglas Democrats and the extreme Southern Democrats divided. The majority named Douglas for President on a popular sovereignty platform. The extreme minority named John C. Breckinridge, demanding a code for the protection of slavery in all territories.

Buchanan had used every resource of his Administration to destroy Douglas, distributing patronage among enemies of the Little Giant, and striving to manipulate the election of delegates. In the end he had failed. The great body of the Democratic Party was behind Douglas, while almost universal disgust was felt for the part Buchanan had played in splitting the party. It was well understood that most supporters of Breckinridge wished to maintain what they called "Southern rights" even if this meant secession. Yet the unofficial headquarters of the Breckinridge campaign were in Buchanan's offices in the White House. It became plain that Breckinridge would run far behind Douglas, and would carry no States outside the slave area. It also became plain that Lincoln would win.

A later cartoon of 1860, "Compromise Doctors," shows Buchanan as a woman, beside a bed on which lies the snake Slavery. Doctors stand about, lettered Crittenden's Amendment, Mexico, Central America, and Cape Horn. Buchanan speaks: "Doctor, my darling child is very sick. I have kindly nursed it for four years. I took it to Kansas for its health, but the vile inhabitants gave it a severe blow in the head." One doctor replies: "Your child will die if you keep it confined; let it have a journey to Mexico or a voyage to Cuba." And two schoolboys speak up: "Charlie, these old quacks are preparing plenty of business to do when we are men."

THE IRREPRESSIBLE CONFLICT; OR, THE REPUBLICAN BARGE IN DANGER

PUBLISHED BY CURRIER & IVES
[1860]

RIVALRIES WERE KEEN in the Republican Party. This cartoon neatly hits off the process by which William H. Seward, foremost leader of the forces opposed to slavery extension, was deprived of the nomination he had expected. Horace Greely and Francis P. Blair throw him overboard, while Lincoln seizes the helm. Seward's followers thought that he had earned the nomination. On the first ballot in the Chicago Convention he had 173½ votes to Lincoln's 102. In Thurlow Weed he had an astute campaign manager. But actually Seward was less "available" than some men of lesser reputation. His speech on the "irrepressible conflict" between slavery and freedom, and his defense of a "higher law" than the Constitution, had made a host of voters regard him as unsafe. Greeley, once his political partner, had become his enemy, and Blair, always a lover of moderation, wanted a more cautious man. But to plenty of conservative voters Lincoln, known for his "house divided" speech and his opposition to the entry of slavery into new Territories, was not much better. The cartoonist represents Brother Jonathan, not yet displaced as a symbol by Uncle Sam, suggesting that the party get rid of its tenderness for the Negro.

Other cartoons of the time touched upon Republican differences. But the differences did not count. With Seward, Chase, Bates and Cameron all loyally supporting Lincoln, the party drove on to victory.

THE POLITICAL RAIL SPLITTER

PUBLISHED BY J. LEACH, N. Y.
[1860]

WE ARE IN THE TURMOIL of the 1860 campaign. The Democrats and the Constitutional Unionists (who nominated John Bell and Edward Everett) are anxious to persuade voters that the election of Lincoln will rive the Union asunder. This cartoon attributes to Lincoln the same "irrepressible conflict" sentiments that Seward had expressed. Greeley has tripped Seward up, and Lincoln (who always denied that he thought disunion inevitable, though he had proclaimed in his house-divided speech of June 16, 1858, that the government must eventually become all slave or all free) is driving the Seward wedge deeper. In mild fashion, for cartoonists generally avoided a strong pro-slavery or anti-slavery position, the drawing hints at the Negro question.

PROGRESSIVE DEMOCRACY—PROSPECT OF A SMASH UP

PUBLISHED BY CURRIER & IVES
[1860]

DEMOCRATIC SCHISM made a Republican victory inevitable. This Currier & Ives print shows the Democratic wagon, representing the two platforms of the two Democratic candidates, stalled on the railroad tracks, with a team of mules at each end, pulling in opposite directions. A Tammany brave (a "squatter sovereign") whips up the Douglas-Johnson team, and Buchanan exhorts the Breckinridge-Lane pair of mules to pull harder. Lincoln's eight-wheel "Equal Rights" engine, with clanging bell and shrieking whistle, is hard upon them. This is a cartoon of the ordinary Currier & Ives type, a type which makes us wonder whether the artists evolved the idea themselves, or had it given them, perhaps by the lithographic firm. But it accurately predicted the result. Though Lincoln's popular vote was only 1,866,452 as against 2,815,617 for his various opponents, he had 180 electoral votes against 72 for Breckinridge, 39 for Bell, and 12 for Douglas. The artist might have shown another train coming down the track—the train of secession. Lincoln received not a single electoral vote in the South, and in ten Southern States not a single ballot was cast for him, for his name did not appear on the voting lists. "The die is cast!" exclaimed many Southerners when they heard the result.

Another review of the situation in this campaign is offered in "Storming the Castle. 'Old Abe' on Guard" (Currier & Ives), one of the comparatively few strongly pro-Lincoln cartoons of the year. Lincoln, in "wide-awake" garb (oilskin cape, used by marchers in political parades to protect their clothes from drippings of their kerosene torches), says: "Ah! ha! Gentlemen! You needn't think to catch me napping; for I am a regular wide awake." Douglas fails to open the White House door with keys "Regular Nom.", "Nonintervention" and "Nebraska Bill," and Buchanan tries to pull up Breckinridge through a window. However, in such general, inclusive summaries the publishers of cartoons apparently often "played safe" by being non-committal. So we get in this same year "The Undecided Prize Fight," with Douglas and Lincoln in the ring, Lincoln attended by a Negro. The black man pops up in a number of Lincoln cartoons, such as two Currier & Ives productions, "The Nigger in the Woodpile" (a title well indicative of the uncomfortable presence of the slavery issue) and "An Heir to the Throne," in which latter Barnum's weak-minded "What is it" is proposed as a worthy successor to Lincoln in carrying out his policies.

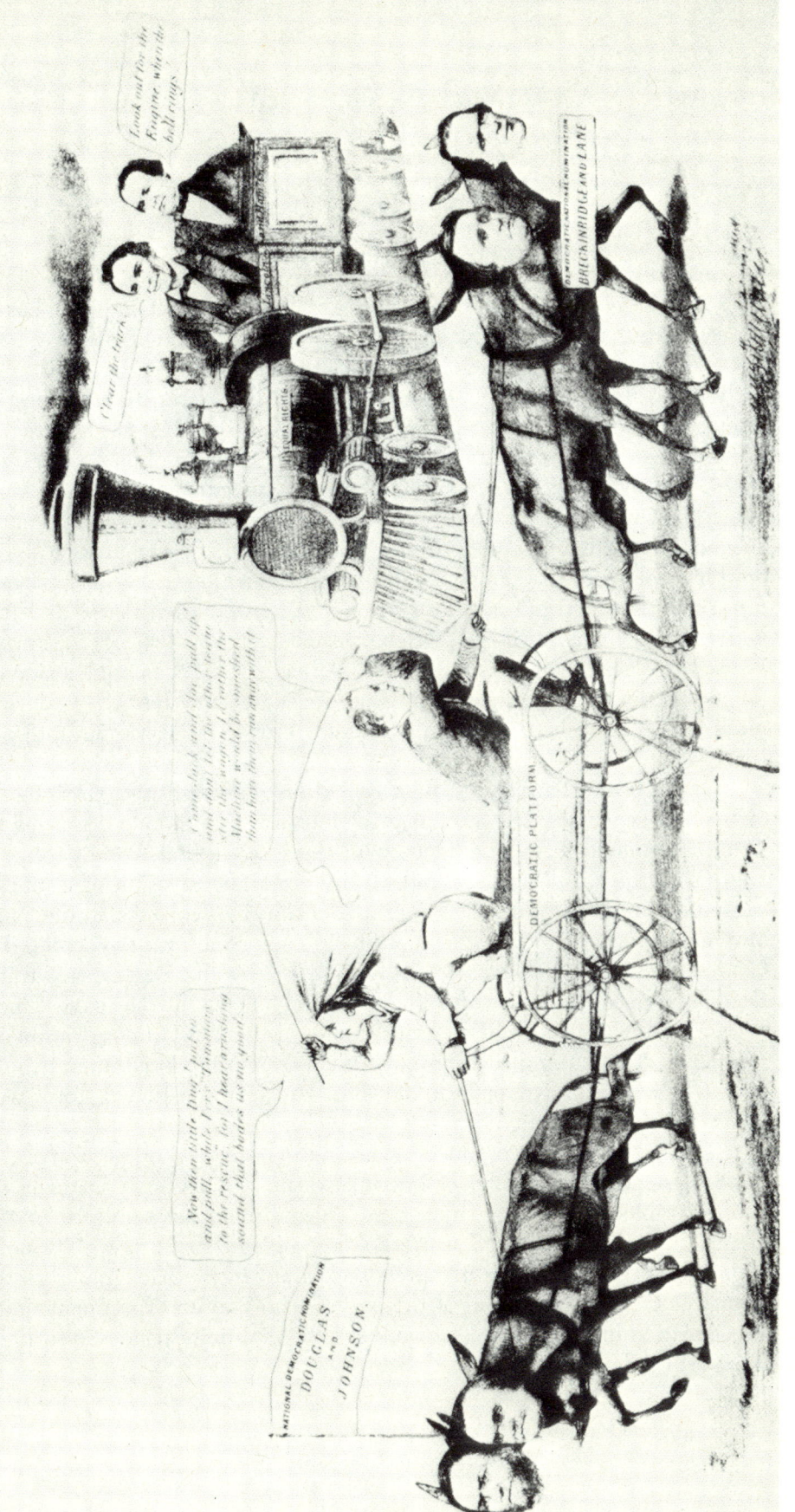

THE NATIONAL GAME. THREE "OUTS" AND ONE "RUN"

PUBLISHED BY CURRIER & IVES
[1860]

AT LAST A NEW IDEA! The principal interest of this drawing lies in its use of baseball in place of the eternal horse-race, cock-fight, or boxing-match; though the likenesses are all good. Founded, as early hand-books of rules prove, on the old English game of rounders, baseball by the early fifties had taken on its essential form of later days, though the sides often consisted of eleven or even fifteen men. At first it was played in scratch fashion; then clubs were organized and efforts made to obtain expert men; by 1858 it was possible to set up the National Association of Baseball Players. When the Civil War broke out, almost every town and city had its team, and large crowds attended competitive matches. Yet this cartoon suggests that the phraseology of the game was still strange. Such terms as fair ball, home run, short-stop, and put-out are surrounded by quotation marks as if they had the charm of novelty. (Indeed, as late as Nov. 25, 1865, *Harper's Weekly* still used the marks for "nine.") Already, it will be noted, a side that failed to score was "skunked." Prints of later date show that the underhand pitch, as distinguished from the overhand throw, was in vogue until after 1870.

Of the beaten candidates, John Bell at first opposed the secession of his own State, Tennessee. But when fighting began at Fort Sumter, he urged that Tennessee should form an alliance with the seceded States and defend the South by arms at all hazards and at any cost. The invasion of Tennessee caused him to flee to the lower South. Breckinridge remained in the Senate until midsummer of 1861, opposing Lincoln's war policy. He then entered the Confederate army, and was formally expelled by the Senate as a traitor. Douglas pursued a course that did him undying credit. He gave Lincoln every possible assistance in the critical days of the new Administration, and when the President called for 75,000 volunteers after Fort Sumter, he exclaimed, "I would have made it 200,000!" His death on June 3, 1861, was a heavy blow to the Union.

The 1860 campaign produced many cartoons, a good proportion of them not too friendly to Lincoln, or but lukewarm, if not openly critical. That stumbling-block, the Negro question, creeps into many; indeed, in "The Great Exhibition of 1860," Seward, holding a Negro child, says: "It's no use trying to keep me and the 'Irrepressible' infant in the background, for we are really the head and front of the party." The War and the Emancipation Proclamation brought some change; yet anti-Abolition cartoons appeared in the North as late as 1864.

LITTLE BO-PEEP AND HER FOOLISH SHEEP
PUBLISHED BY T. W. STRONG
[1861]

BUCHANAN'S ADMINISTRATION dragged to its end in weakness and confusion—almost in despair. This wood engraving, issued, as "Strong's Dime Caricatures.—No. 2," by the publisher of the comic paper *Yankee Notions*, graphically describes the folly of South Carolina and her errant sisters, the consternation of Columbia, and the cowardly uselessness of Buchanan, who, as a shepherd dog, scuttles off with tail between his legs. South Carolina seceded on December 20th, 1860, and Mississippi, Florida and Alabama on the 9th, 10th, and 11th of January. For a time some people hoped that Buchanan might play a resolute role. The prospect for this brightened after his Cabinet was reorganized to include a number of strong Union men, Jeremiah S. Black becoming Secretary of State, and Edwin M. Stanton Attorney-General. But as Douglas had contemptuously told Buchanan a couple of years earlier, Andrew Jackson was dead—as this cartoon shows him. When Buchanan sent the *Star of the West* in January to reinforce Fort Sumter, the ship was driven back by the fire of South Carolina cannon. A stronger President might have pressed the issue. Buchanan simply marked time, doing nothing further to aid Fort Sumter, and hoping that one of the schemes of conciliation and compromise might prove effective. His temporizing position was indicated in the lithograph "South Carolina's Ultimatum," in which Governor Pickens holds a fuse to the cannon "Peace Maker"; Buchanan pleads: "Don't fire! till I get out of office."

To the fact that many Southerners wished for a compromise the cartoon refers by showing Virginia in a pleading attitude. The legislature of Virginia, in fact, invited the States to send representatives to a peace convention in Washington on February 4th. Twenty-one States accepted, and their delegates, with ex-President Tyler acting as chairman, deliberated long and anxiously. They finally recommended an amendment to the Constitution that would make the old Missouri Compromise line of 36′ 30″ the boundary line between slave and free Territories, and that would also require concurrent majorities of both slave-state and free-state senators for the acquisition of any new territory. But neither this nor Senator Crittenden's proposed compromise (also making 36′ 30″ the line between free and slave soil) won sufficient favor. The secession movement had gone too far and extremists on both sides objected to the two plans.

Another cartoon of the time, "South Carolina Topsy in a Fix" (one of only two that have been found referring to Mrs. Stowe's *Uncle Tom's Cabin*) presents Columbia with an American flag in her lap. She is addressing South Carolina severely: "So, Topsey, you're at the bottom of this piece of wicked work—picking stars out of this sacred Flag! . . . I'll just hand you over to the new overseer, Uncle Abe. He'll fix you!"

THE "SECESSION MOVEMENT"

PUBLISHED BY CURRIER & IVES
[1861]

ONCE STARTED, the secession movement could not be stopped. After the four leaders, Georgia voted on January 19 to leave the Union; Louisiana on January 26; Texas on February 1. On February 4 representatives of six of the fifteen slave States met at Montgomery to organize a Southern Confederacy. This body, calling itself a provisional legislature, named a provisional President—the aristocratic Jefferson Davis, on whose shoulders in the Senate had fallen the mantle of John C. Calhoun. The cartoonist rather curiously discriminates between Georgia and her associates. It is true that Georgia, where the influence of Unionists like Alexander H. Stephens and Herschel V. Johnson was strong, had a large minority opposed to secession. Johnson proposed that instead of leaving the Union, Georgia should lay down a set of conditions on which she would remain in it, and present them to the other States. But this suggestion came to nothing, and the Georgia convention voted for secession 208 to 89.

Some of the speeches inserted in the mouths of the Southern States are allusions to past history. It was all too true that Mississippi had once defaulted on her debt. It was true that some Floridians along the keys were supposed to make a living by wrecking ships. But the best hit in this animated, though poorly drawn, lithograph is the speech put in the mouth of Alabama: "We go it blind, 'Cotton is King.'" That blind faith in cotton as an article of prime necessity to the rest of the world made many Southerners believe their new confederation could not fail.

The storm having broken loose, our cartoonists began to show a little more energy in the face of an accomplished fact. Confronted by a condition, not a theory (to use Cleveland's phrase of a later date), they became a bit more bravely outspoken. This changing attitude is illustrated in a group of cartoons, such as the one here reproduced, "The Great Disunion Serpent," and others. "The Disunited States" (six Southern States, each with its own special interests and demands) was issued by Currier & Ives, on one of the occasions when they spoke right out loud. However, really powerful cartoons, usually the result of strong convictions expressed with competent and vigorous artistry, were not yet generally forthcoming.

THE INSIDE TRACK

BY HENRY L. STEPHENS

[1861]

Who would control the new Administration? Many thought that it would be Secretary of State William H. Seward. Weed, intensely disappointed by Seward's failure to win the nomination, doubtless assumed that Seward, because of long experience in public affairs, and commanding influence within the party, would take the controlling place in the government. Here he says to the President Elect: "Trust to my friend Seward." Seward himself, in his memorandum to the President of April 1, reproached Lincoln for lack of any firm policy; declared that somebody must take responsibility for formulating a plan and carrying it out; intimated that he would be glad to do so; and proposed that the United States demand categorical explanations from several European powers on the question of intervention, and if satisfactory answers were not received, open war against France and Spain. Lincoln quietly put this foolish memorandum away; the country did not learn of it till long after the war. The President was from the beginning full master of his Administration.

DARING LEAP

BY HENRY L. STEPHENS

[1861]

As the Lincoln Administration set to work, nothing gave the North more comfort than the unhesitating adherence of Stephen A. Douglas to the cause of the Union. When running for the Presidency in 1860, he was asked at Norfolk whether he would advise the South to secede if Lincoln were elected, and whether he would support the North in opposing secession by force. His answer was that the duty of the President was to execute the laws; he himself would "do all in my power to aid the government of the United States in maintaining supremacy of the laws against all resistance to them, come from what quarter it might." This cartoon anticipated the action which Douglas took immediately after the firing on Fort Sumter. He pledged full support to the Administration; then, going to Illinois, threw himself into the task of rallying that State to the flag of the Union. His influence contributed powerfully to unity of effort behind Lincoln. Douglas was a martyr to national duty, for in his efforts he brought on the complication of maladies which killed him.

DARING LEAP.
MADE BY THE CELEBRATED ACROBAT LITTLE GIANT.

BREAKING THAT "BACKBONE"

BY BENJAMIN DAY

[1862]

BY MIDSUMMER OF 1862, with the failure of McClellan before Richmond, the strength and toughness of the Confederacy were plain to the blindest. The South was indeed a "gyascutis" with the stiffest backbone ever seen. How could it be broken? McClellan's strategy had achieved nothing, and his army was brought back from the Peninsula to its old post in front of Washington. Henry W. Halleck's very uncertain "skill" was tried. This veteran army man, who had served in the Mexican War and brought out a textbook on military science, was made military adviser to the President, with the title of general-in-chief. But he gave far less time to broad planning than to details of raising and equipping troops, and was nearly if not quite useless. The heavy hammer of Stanton's draft law of 1862 counted for something, but was not heavy enough. This original draft act, in fact, simply provided for using the State systems of conscripting men into the militia, and atoning for any deficiencies by Federal regulations. When Pope was defeated at Second Bull Run on August 29–30, none of the Union weapons seemed strong enough.

But one resource, in addition to heavier armies and fresh commanders, remained—the Emancipation Proclamation. For months Lincoln had been urged to raise the war to a higher moral level and strike terror to the South by making the liberation of the slaves one of its avowed objects. Greeley had scolded him in his editorial "The Prayer of Twenty Millions," and Lincoln had replied with calm argument. He was waiting until the time was ripe —until a decree of emancipation would mean something, and not look like the Pope's futile "bull against the comet." As early as July 13, 1862, he had concluded, as he told Secretaries Seward and Welles, that an emancipation proclamation was absolutely essential to the saving of the Union. He drafted it, and laid it aside until the Northern armies could win a victory. In September Lee's invasion was turned back at the battle of Antietam. The time had come, and the proclamation was issued, to become effective at the beginning of the following year. In more than one way this great document did help to break the backbone of the Confederacy. It raised the determination of the North; it placed the government in a better light before Europe, making foreign intervention more difficult; and it dismayed many Southerners. It shortened the conflict.

Day had a freedom in drawing not characteristic of Currier & Ives lithographs as a whole. Other cartoons dealt with the same subject. One pictured "The Grand Sweepstakes for 1862 won by Emancipation"; another presented emancipation as "The Great Remedy," or "Lincoln's Blackstrap."

DISSOLVING VIEWS OF RICHMOND

ANONYMOUS
[1862]

EVEN AFTER BULL RUN, Northern hopes of early victory ran high. When McClellan advanced on Richmond with 100,000 troops, the Washington authorities expected a decisive blow. But, alas, in the battles of the "Seven Days" the Northern forces were fought to a standstill. The final struggle at Malvern Hill left McClellan exhausted. He did his utmost to lay the blame upon the Administration, which had detached a large body of men from his command for the defense of Washington; but the main responsibility was his own. As the people of the North read their heavy casualty lists, profound discouragement seized many communities.

This is the third of four neatly drawn Confederate prints exploiting the Union discomfiture. The first showed the boastful advance. This presents the retreat disguised as a "strategic movement." The satire is not sufficiently vigorous to make powerful cartoons. But the situation is rendered laughable enough from the Southern point of view. Such drawings make one regret that Confederate caricatures were not more numerous.

WORSHIP OF THE NORTH

BY ADALBERT J. VOLCK ("BLADA")
[1863]

AS THE WAR CONTINUED and casualty lists mounted, feeling on both sides grew more bitter. In debates over the slavery issue the South had frequently expressed reprobation of Northern civilization as materialistic, productive of hypocrisy and cant, and full of crazy "isms." This savage caricature makes use of this thesis. Lincoln, with the head of a clown, presides at a bloody sacrifice of the nation's youth on an altar built up of Negro Worship, Spirit Rapping, Free Love, Witch-Burning, Socialism, Atheism, and Rationalism, on the foundation-stone of Puritanism. Above the altar a Negro sits apotheosized. H. W. Beecher holds a dripping knife, Greeley a censer, and Sumner a torch. Butler, his knapsack stuffed with loot, exults in the scene. The statue labelled "Pray for us" is of St. Osawatomie, or John Brown. A crowd of fat contractors marches with the banner "More Blood."

Volck, foremost among Southern cartoonists of the time, issued a series of "Confederate War Etchings." From the artistic point of view his work has been somewhat overrated, but his satire was stinging.

THE GRAVE OF THE UNION,
OR MAJOR JACK DOWNING'S DREAM
"DRAWN BY ZEKE"
[1864]

To meet the disloyal practices of Southern sympathizers, even the mild and just Lincoln had to adopt methods that were dictatorial in character and ran counter to Anglo-Saxon traditions of civil rights. Congress on July 31, 1861, put a Conspiracies Act on the statute books, and nearly a year later passed a stern law for the punishment of treason. But the courts were reluctant to proceed under these acts, and Attorney-General Bates was still more reluctant to assemble evidence and carry on prosecutions. The government, properly or improperly, used more direct means. Lincoln in September, 1862, issued a proclamation directing trial by courts martial or military commissions of all persons who impeded the draft, discouraged enlistments, or committed other disloyal acts. Many thousands were arrested. They were not permitted the right of habeas corpus, but were held in jail until tried. One authority fixes the whole number at 38,000; it was probably not so large. The most famous arrest was that of Clement L. Vallandigham, Copperhead leader of Ohio, who in 1863 was thrown into a "military bastille" by General Ambrose E. Burnside because he had made a speech in which he declared that the war was not being fought for the Union, but to liberate the Negro and enslave the white man. When a military commission sentenced Vallandigham to imprisonment for the duration of the war, Lincoln commuted the sentence to banishment within the Confederate lines. Lincoln and his associates were violently attacked by the Democrats for their extra-legal measures. Such leaders as Horatio Seymour declared that if the President were not checked, liberty and the Constitution would be made worthless. It was in reply to such criticisms that Lincoln, explaining that many of the arrests were really "preventive," asked his famous question: "Must I shoot a simple-minded soldier boy who deserts, while I must not touch a hair of a wily agitator who induces him to desert?"

This cartoon, an example of criticism sure to arise under restrictions in wartime, is self-explanatory, and states the Seymour-Vallandigham position with a good deal of force. Lincoln, Sumner, and Greeley are burying the Constitution, Free Speech, the Habeas Corpus, and the Union. In the background are War Democrats who abet Secretary Stanton in the process—General John Cochrane of New York; General Ben Butler of Massachusetts, General Thomas F. Meagher, head of the famous Irish Brigade; and Daniel D. Dickinson, who had been an aspirant for the Democratic nomination in 1860, but supported the Union so vigorously that he went over to the Republican Party. "Jack Downing" was the comic Yankee character created in the thirties by Seba Smith.

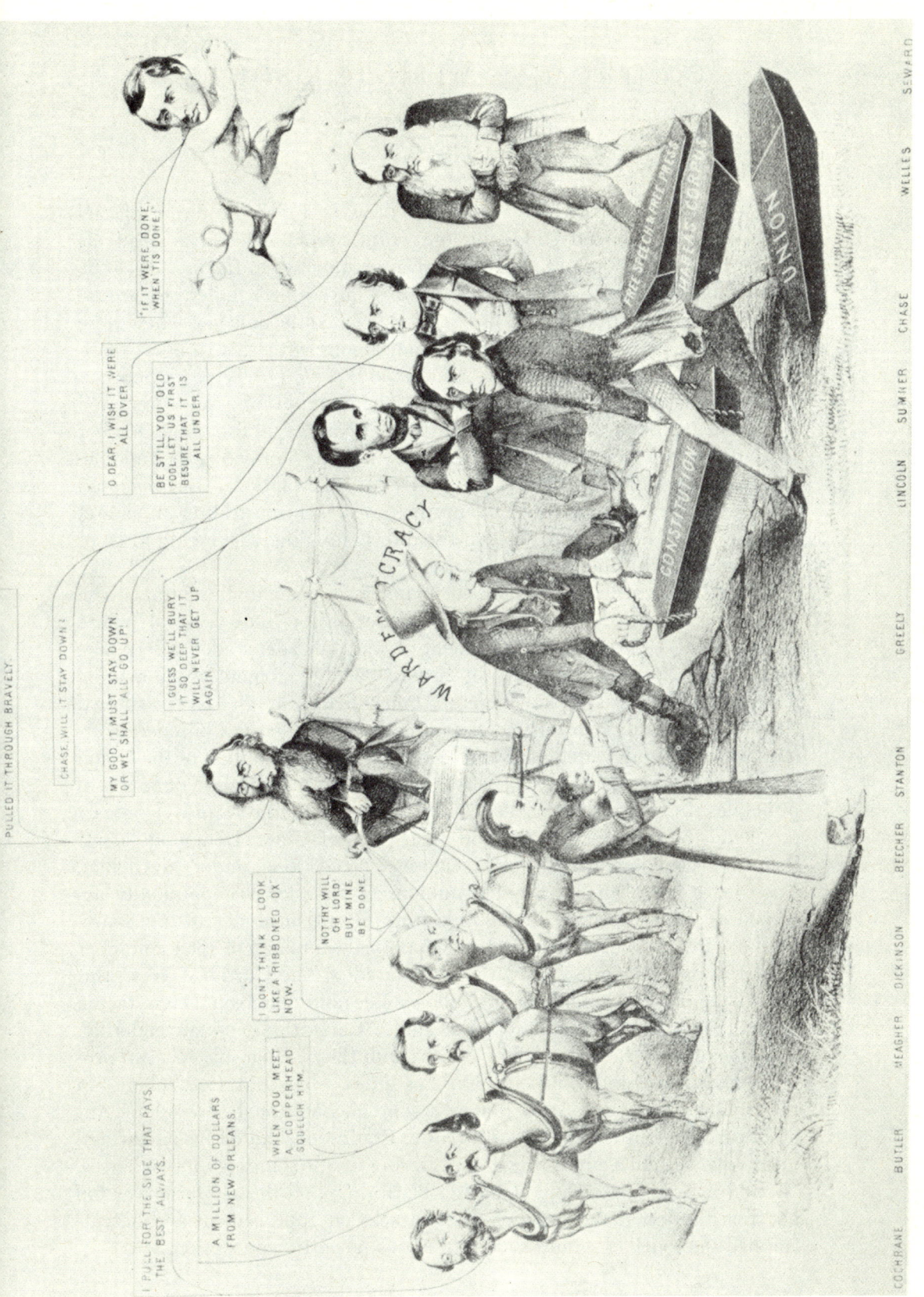

COMPROMISE WITH THE SOUTH

BY THOMAS NAST

[1864]

As the presidential canvass of 1864 drew to a close, a master of cartooning stepped suddenly into public prominence. Nast had attracted some attention by his patriotic drawings in *Harper's Weekly*. "His emblematic cartoons," said Lincoln, "have never failed to arouse enthusiasm and patriotism, and have always seemed to come just when these articles were getting scarce." He became famous with this design, "dedicated to the Chicago Convention," which the *Weekly* published on September 3. The Republican National Committee had millions of copies circulated as a campaign document. A second cartoon of Nast's, published on October 15, reiterated the general theme of this drawing—the betrayal of the republic and the much-suffering soldiers by the Democratic platform. But being an intricate combination of about twenty pictures, each illustrating an extract from the hated document, it lacked the direct, stinging, convincing force of "Compromise with the South."

The Democratic Convention had laid itself open to this attack. The platform condemned the Lincoln Administration for "four years of failure to restore the Union by the experiment of war," and demanded a stoppage of hostilities "to the end that at the earliest possible moment peace may be restored on the basis of the Federal Union of the States." Every shrewd citizen knew that if an armistice were proclaimed while the Confederate armies were still undefeated, it would lead rather to a dissolution of the Union forever, or to its restoration on terms that would mean a triumph of Southern principles. In vain did McClellan insist that if elected he would vigorously prosecute the war. In vain did the great mass of Union Democrats assert that they would demand such a vigorous prosecution under McClellan. Nast drove home an idea, which millions of Americans undoubtedly accepted as valid, that the Chicago platform meant surrender to the South. Of the many cartoons produced by the political campaign of 1864 a number on the Republican side deal with the same idea. The Currier & Ives print "The True Peace Commissioners" shows Lee and Jefferson Davis facing Grant, Sherman, Sheridan and Farragut. "Can't think of surrendering, gentlemen," says Lee, "but allow me through the Chicago platform to propose an armistice and a suspension of hostilities." "That's it, Lee," chimes in Davis. But Grant replies: "I demand your unconditional surrender." Another cartoon, "Little Mac's double feat of Equitation," hit off his embarrassment very well. In a circus ring, he was trying to ride standing on two horses, "Letter of Acceptance" and "Chicago Platform"—and the platform was too far from the letter. But none of these attacks on appeasement and defeatism had the touch of genius shown in Nast's powerful conception.

OUR FOREIGN RELATIONS

BY A. HOCHSTEIN

[1864]

IN SYMBOLISM this cartoon is decidedly vague and general. The American eagle stands triumphant on the rock of Liberty, pinning down the dragon "Treason" and "Secession," the latter shrieking "Help us!" Discomfiture is shown by the Gallic cock, the timid monkey Napoleon III, the angry British lion, and the Canadian unicorn. The cartoon appealed to sentiments of nationalism and resentment which Americans felt when in the closing phases of the Civil War they thought of their foreign relations. The resentment was largely unjustified. The North felt deeply the depredations of the Confederate cruiser *Alabama*, built in England and armed on the high seas, and other vessels of similar character. But the motives of the British Ministry seem to have been fair; they bore no ill will toward the United States, and when the *Alabama* escaped from British jurisdiction as a result of official delays and unhappy accidents, at least four Cabinet members in London were deeply regretful. The British masses were with the North, even in the starving Lancashire areas where stoppage of cotton shipments had occasioned great distress. This fact the cartoonist, who suggests that cotton was the main-spring of British policy, ignores. If Great Britain and France had recognized the independence of the Confederacy, or made a stern demand for an armistice, the South would almost certainly have established itself as a separate nation. Practically all danger of this passed away in the fall of 1862, when news of Antietam and the Emancipation Proclamation reached Europe. Napoleon III was more hostile to the North than the British Ministry; but he had to reckon with a strong feeling in France against slavery, and he had no choice but to follow the British lead.

Several other cartoons of the period deal with foreign relations. A lithograph entitled "John Bull makes a Discovery," shows John Bull with one hand on the woolly head of a Negro, and the other holding a fluff of cotton. He remarks: "Well, yes!—It is certain that cotton is more useful to me than wool!!" The intimation is that Great Britain let her interest in cotton supplies outweigh her philanthropic hopes for freeing the slave; which was the opposite of the fact. Another, "John Bull in a Quandary," shows John Bull acutely conscious of the burden of his national debt of four billion dollars; the Czar cynically remarks: "Aha, the day may yet come when Sebastopol will be revenged." Russia had a long tradition of friendship with the United States, and her foreign minister, Prince Gortchakov, freely manifested his sympathy with the North during the Civil War. Late in 1863, Russian squadrons paid friendly visits to New York and San Francisco, and were cordially received.

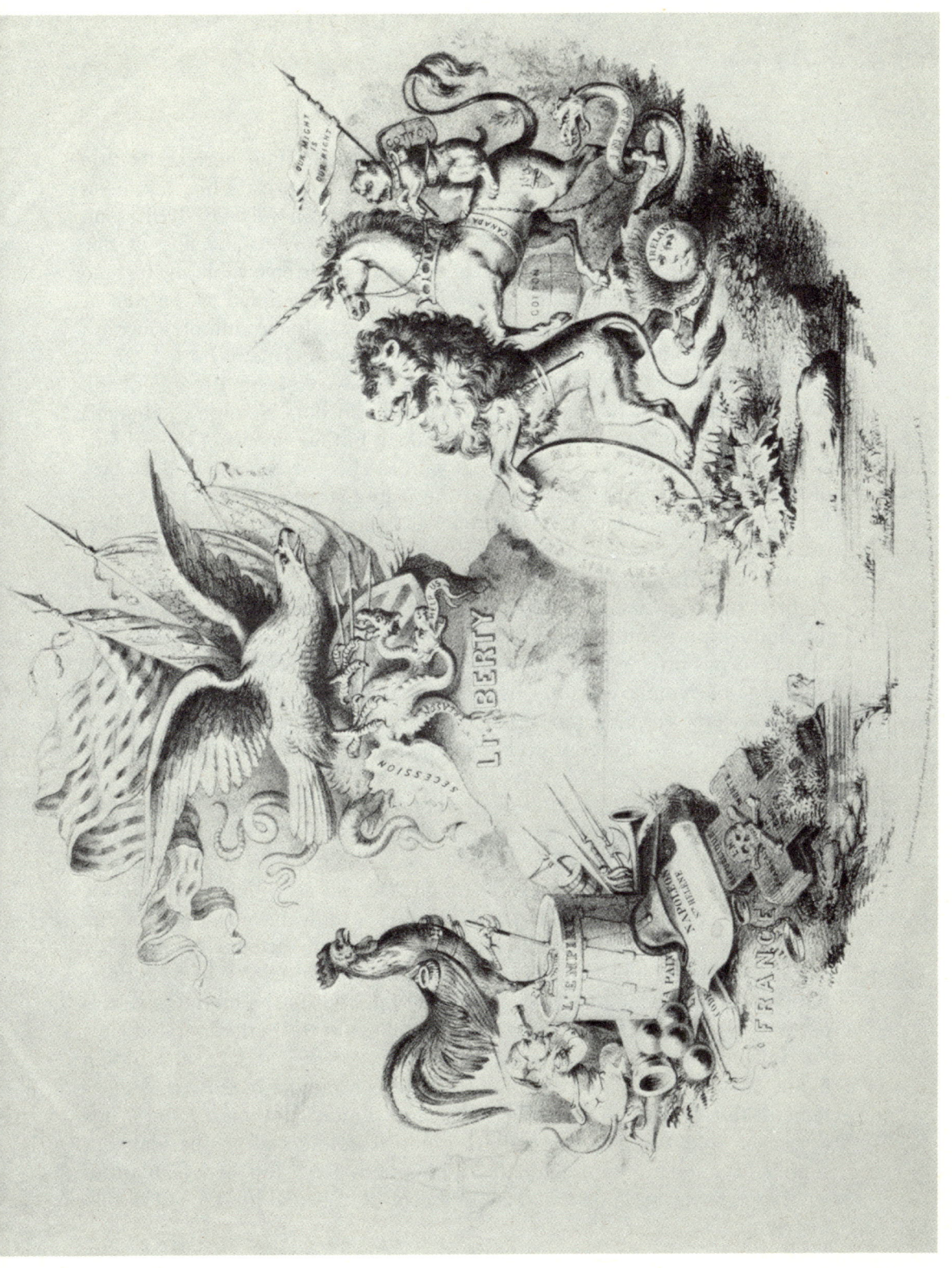

RUNNING THE "MACHINE"

PUBLISHED BY CURRIER & IVES

[1864]

THIS VIOLENT ATTACK on the Lincoln Administration derives its title from a letter which Edwin M. Stanton, then in private life, had been indiscreet enough to write James Buchanan on July 26, 1861, soon after Bull Run. Speaking of the battle, he raged: "The imbecility of this Administration culminated in that catastrophe; an irretrievable misfortune and national disgrace never to be forgotten are to be added to the ruin of all peaceful pursuits and national bankruptcy, as the result of Lincoln's 'running the machine' for five months." In a letter to General John A. Dix a few weeks earlier Stanton had denounced "the weakness and panic of the Administration, and the painful imbecility of Lincoln." Stanton's judgment in such matters was poor, and his pen reckless. But opponents of the Administration naturally made capital of his words. This cartoon shows Secretary of the Treasury Fessenden directing the manufacture of a flood of greenback money (altogether, $432,000,000 was issued during the war); Welles, who before the war had been a newspaper editor of inland Connecticut, making a ludicrous blunder in moving ships; Stanton happy over the slightest success; Lincoln reminded of a good story; and contractors eagerly demanding more funds. Seward's arbitrary arrests are not overlooked. The habeas corpus privilege had been suspended, and the Secretary of State put in charge of summary arrests by the executive authority. Seward had an effective secret service organization, and a way of cramming prisoners into Fort Lafayette without informing anybody upon the government's case against them.

The cartoon has a certain rude directness, but it is stiff and poorly drawn, and its ideas are elementary. The war called for caricature of a slashing type, and offered plenty of texts for it, but unfortunately cartoonists of genuine power were not yet to be found. We had no Gillray, no Daumier, no Tenniel—for Nast made his real emergence only near the end of the conflict, and published but one really remarkable war cartoon. As one of the editors of this volume remarks in *American Graphic Art:* "When we draw the line under the long Civil War column, and add up the total, the sum is not very impressive qualitatively. The possibilities of the period were perhaps not fully grasped by our caricaturists. In fact, we had no commanding figure among them." The treatment of the contractors in this drawing is tame. Elihu Vedder, in a small "comic" contributed to *Vanity Fair,* struck a sharper note when he presented a group of soldiers using the blankets, supplied by shoddy contractors, as fishing-nets. Such hits at irregularities were rare, however, and were done in the spirit of genial humor, not of telling satire.

THE COMMANDER-IN-CHIEF CONCILIATING THE SOLDIER'S VOTES ON THE BATTLEFIELD

ANONYMOUS
[1864]

THE PRESIDENTIAL CONTEST of 1864 seemed doubtful until the early part of September. Lincoln himself, in a secret memorandum, stated that "it seems exceedingly probable that this Administration will not be reelected," and that "it will be my duty to so coöperate with the President-elect as to save the Union between the election and the inauguration; as he will have secured his election on such ground that he cannot possibly save it afterwards." The Democrats, who at Chicago nominated George Brinton McClellan, made the most of the awful costs of the war. Three years had passed; hundreds of thousands of the nation's best young men, North and South, had died on the battlefield, hundreds of thousands had been mutilated; Grant in Virginia seemed at a standstill, and the fighting from the Wilderness to Cold Harbor had cost nearly sixty thousand men; victory appeared as distant as ever. Confronted with this terrible slaughter, declared the Democrats, Lincoln was capable of nothing better than another of his vulgar jokes. Arrangements had been made for taking the vote of the soldiers in the field—and it looked as if Lincoln might need it. But the President's popularity was greater than most observers supposed, while the war was going better for the North than its superficial aspects indicated. The Virginia fighting that cost Grant so heavily was also costly to the Confederates—and Grant could replace his men, while Lee could not. Sherman was moving irresistibly forward, and on September 3rd the country was electrified by the news that he had occupied Atlanta. The elections that month in Maine and Vermont gave huge Republican majorities. On September 22d Frémont, nominated by dissenting Republicans as head of a third ticket, withdrew. From that moment it was clear that Lincoln and his Union Party (both Union Democrats and Union Republicans had joined behind him, and the Vice-Presidential nominee, Andrew Johnson, was a Democrat) would win.

Cartoons were numerous during this campaign. The present one, bitter but amateurishly executed, was perhaps the best produced on the "Copperhead" side. It has more vigor than another, for example, which is entitled "The True Way." In this Lincoln and Jefferson Davis are tugging at opposite ends of a map of the United States. McClellan catches each by the collar, and ejaculates, "The Union must be preserved at all hazards!" But by 1864 attempts to suggest that Lincoln was careless of the Union, or that it could be saved by compromise measures, were as absurd as efforts to suggest that Lincoln was not deeply stricken by the war's cost in life and human anguish.

"SPOONS" AS FALSTAFF MUSTERING THE IMPEACHMENT MANAGERS

BY THOMAS WORTH

[1868]

THE MOST DRAMATIC EVENT of the Reconstruction period, Andrew Johnson's impeachment, was also the most discreditable to the Radical Republicans who controlled the national government. That no real foundation for impeachment existed, and that it was based merely upon party motives and personal dislike, has been the unanimous verdict of historians. The managers of the impeachment were of course members of the House. Their names (they once took the trouble to get themselves photographed in a body for the benefit of posterity) were Thaddeus Stevens of Pennsylvania, Benjamin F. Butler of Massachusetts, John A. Bingham of Ohio, Thomas Williams of Pennsylvania, James F. Wilson of Iowa, George S. Boutwell of Massachusetts, and John A. Logan of Illinois. The real leader in the procedure was Thaddeus Stevens, vindictive hater of "rebels," who had stated in Congress that he meant to give the remainder of his life to the "punishment of traitors," and who felt he had been opposed too long by President Johnson. The man who presented the articles of impeachment to the House was the narrow-minded partisan Boutwell, who had the assurance to praise the "artistic construction" of this clumsy, repetitious, and unconvincing indictment. But for natural reasons the cartoonist made crosseyed, unscrupulous Ben Butler the center of his composition. He looked more like Falstaff than any other, he was an object of suspicion and amusement even among Radicals, and his military record possessed some comic touches. Down into the eighties cartoonists labelled him "Spoons" because it was believed that no bit of silver had been safe in New Orleans while he ruled that city. Butler made the opening argument for the prosecution before the Senate. He was followed by Thad Stevens, who was too feeble to complete the reading of his manuscript, but who was as savage as ever. Any Senator who voted for acquittal, he declared, would consign himself "to the gibbet of everlasting obloquy." The breakdown of the impeachment was a heavier blow to Stevens than to anyone else.

There are numerous allusive touches in the cartoon; for example, the tailor's shears stuck in Andrew Johnson's belt. Thomas Worth was known chiefly as a general illustrator and caricaturist, but he did a few cartoons. Currier & Ives had previously issued a somewhat similar caricature, "The Smelling Committee," which satirized the House committee under James M. Ashley of Ohio that had made a mean-spirited search for evidence against President Johnson. The President, in this Reconstruction period, was attacked with special bitterness by Nast.

RECONSTRUCTION, OR "A WHITE MAN'S GOVERNMENT"

PUBLISHED BY CURRIER & IVES

[1868]

THIS PRINT IS ONE which the Union League Clubs both North and South must have hung in their rooms with warm approval. The Reconstruction legislation of 1867, placing the South temporarily under military rule and demanding the erection of new State governments on the basis of Negro suffrage and partial white disfranchisement, had placed the colored man and his white allies, the Carpetbaggers and scalawags, in control of ten States of the former Confederacy. That the conservative white people of the South regarded this "black and tan" rule or misrule with the deepest disgust goes without saying. They opposed the new regime with every weapon they could grasp—the ballot, the Ku Klux Klan, and unfortunately in many areas with violence. For this attitude they had good reason: the governments of the Radicals (that is, the Carpetbagger, scalawag, and Negro alliance) were spectacularly incompetent, wasteful, and corrupt. Within a few years they piled up enormous debts in most Southern States, and raised taxation to such high levels that many Southern whites lost their lands for failure to pay the charges. The ludicrous yet tragic character of the misgovernment in South Carolina has been described in J. S. Pike's classic book on *The Prostrate State*. Yet South Carolina did not suffer more than Mississippi, where the tax rate in 1874 was fourteen times as high as in 1869, or than Louisiana, where the spoils of offices and contracts were fought over by rival machines. President Grant, after a brief initial show of moderation, supported the Radical regime in the South because it meant Republican votes in Congress and the electoral college, and because his strong sense of respect for order made him antagonistic to the Klan violence. A great many Northerners took the attitude here inculcated—that if the Southern white would only accept Negro equality and work in friendly coöperation with his black brother, they might rapidly regain prosperity together. But the Southern white knew better; he knew that the only hope for order and progress in his section lay in the rapid reëstablishment of his own supremacy. In one State after another he gained control, until by the summer of 1877—the year in which the Federal Government ceased its interference and acquiesced in white control—the entire South had been rewon.

This lithograph is not better drawn than other Currier & Ives productions, and has the same made-to-order quality that characterizes most of them. But its simplicity and unity show that the Currier & Ives establishment was perhaps learning some essential principles of caricature. The point is made not by a clutter of figures standing woodenly about, but by three men only, strongly contrasted in pose and action.

THE MAN OF WORDS. THE MAN OF DEEDS. WHICH DO YOU THINK THE COUNTRY NEEDS?

BY J. CAMERON

[1868]

To a majority of americans in 1868 the choice between Grant and Horatio Seymour was clear. Grant, the strong silent man of Appomattox, had slain the Rebellion and saved the Union; Seymour, "Copperhead" governor of New York, during the draft riots of 1863 had addressed a turbulent crowd from the steps of the City Hall with the words "My friends." The Currier & Ives cartoonist has made the most of the contrast. Such propaganda as this helped to give Grant his not too tremendous majority; he had a popular vote of 3,012,000 against 2,703,000 for Seymour —and if the Negro vote had been deducted, Seymour would have had a lead. The cartoon is somewhat unfair to Seymour. The crowd he addressed in July, 1863, was actually an orderly assemblage; violence that day was three miles away from the City Hall; and he appealed for peace and order. But it cannot be denied that Seymour refused to coöperate with the Lincoln Administration, and that a slightly earlier speech in Albany, attacking Lincoln for alleged infractions of personal liberty, may have helped fan the lawless spirit which brought about the riots.

The many cartoons of 1868 contain some unusually interesting drawings, for the bitterness of the Reconstruction struggle had stimulated party feeling. One rather humorous effort by Thomas Worth, "The Great American Tanner," issued by Currier & Ives (who as usual supplied both parties with ammunition) shows Governor Hoffman of New York, a sachem of Tammany, presenting Horatio Seymour and Frank P. Blair to Grant. "Here, general," he says, "is a couple more hides to be tanned. When will they be done?" And Grant replies: "Well, I'll finish them off early in November." On the other side was a cartoon, entitled "The Precarious Situation," which held more truth than most people then supposed. This anonymous lithograph pictured Grant brandishing a knife "Despotism" (recalling later digs at Grant for supposed dictatorial methods), balanced over Salt River on a rope labelled "Radical Platform," which was held at one end by a Negro and supported at the other by a musket identified as "Military Reconstruction." The Negro, labelled "Negro Supremacy," was saying: "Whar you be, Massa Grant, if I lef' go? Yah, Yah!!" Before Grant finished his eight unfortunate years in the White House, the Negro had let go in all but three States—and the result was the victory of Tilden and the Democratic Party in 1876, though they never gathered the fruits of their triumph.

Cameron, like more than one lithographic artist of his day, apparently took his jobs as they came—horse-racing pictures, cartoons, or what not. Such is not the stuff of which effective cartoonists are made.

A GROUP OF VULTURES WAITING FOR THE STORM TO "BLOW OVER"

BY THOMAS NAST
[1871]

"Blow over" was Mayor A. Oakey Hall's phrase. Here the vultures are waiting—Hall; Sweeny, park commissioner and city chamberlain of New York City; Connolly, the sneak-thief controller; and Tweed himself. Hall had hoped that the storm raised by Nast's cartoons and the New York *Times* exposure of the Tweed Ring would indeed blow over. The *Times* began its articles on July 22, 1871, with carefully tabulated figures proving that millions of dollars had disappeared from the city's treasury. "Who stole the people's money?" demanded Nast's cartoon showing members of the Ring, grouped in a circle, each pointing to his neighbor. The artist's biographer tells us that about this time he was offered a half a million to stop cartooning and go to Europe.

When this picture—a strongly knit composition vividly portraying the desperation of the gang—appeared, a municipal election was imminent. The great question was whether the subordinate officers (for Hall's term had not expired) would be sustained in power or overthrown. They had behind them a powerful machine and thousands of ignorant voters. But Samuel J. Tilden, whose legal acumen was unsurpassed, made a dramatic entry on the scene with evidence, gathered at the Broadway Bank, splendidly supplementing that published in the *Times*. And Nast kept up his fire. On October 7th, in "Stop Thief," he summed up the situation with the Ring scattering in headlong flight. Two days before election he sent a shattering projectile into the Tammany citadel—"The Tammany Tiger loose. What are you going to do about it?", showing the Coliseum, with Tweed and his fellow-conspirators in the imperial box. "But it is only the centre of the amphitheatre that we see," writes Albert Bigelow Paine. "There, with glaring savage eyes and distended jaws, its great, cruel paws crushing down the maimed Republic, we behold the first complete embodiment of the fierce symbol. . . . The creature of rapacity and stripes, whose savage head Tweed had emblazoned on the Tammany banner, had been called into being to rend and destroy him." The city had never seen a challenge more direct and powerful. "What are you going to do about it?"—the ballot-box waited for the answer. On election day the Ring was completely disrupted. Tweed, already arrested, was released only after giving bond for a million dollars. Evidence existed to send him and others to the penitentiary. Nast published after election "Something that did blow over"; a tornado had wrecked Tammany Hall; Tweed caught under the fallen masonry, Sweeny in flight, and "Elegant Oakey" clinging to a single precarious pillar.

Nast's Tweed Ring cartoons form a remarkable example of strongly sustained effort, a ceaseless probing, devastating in effect.

ADDING INSULT TO INJURY
BY THOMAS NAST
[1872]

Not so familiar as some of Nast's other cartoons of the Presidential contest between Grant and Horace Greeley in 1872, this presents in striking fashion Nast's attitude toward Greeley and the forces behind him. It appeared in *Harper's Weekly* May 25, just after the Liberal Republican nomination at Cincinnati. A huge body of Americans agreed with Nast that while Greeley might be a great editor, he was ridiculous as a Presidential nominee. He had abundantly proved during the Civil War that he lacked backbone, consistency, and judgment. His vacillations, his scoldings of the Lincoln Administration, and in the final bloody year his outright defeatism, had disgusted the North. During his long career as editor of the *Tribune* he had let his name become connected with many eccentric beliefs and still more eccentric people; and though his character was above reproach, he was lacking in personal dignity. The cartoonist errs in presenting Carl Schurz as the principal advocate of Greeley—here harshly depicted as a fool's head; for while Schurz was one of the leaders in calling the Liberal Republican Convention as a protest against Grant's incompetency, he was astounded when that body named Greeley instead of Charles Francis Adams or Lyman Trumbull, who would have made far stronger candidates. Schurz was a devout believer in low tariffs, Greeley a strong advocate of high protection. For a time Schurz even thought of bolting the ticket.

Cruel as the cartoon seems (for Greeley was anything but a fool, as his powerful campaign speeches showed, while it was quite improper to identify him in any way with Boss Tweed, or with Jefferson Davis, whom he had merely bailed out of prison), it is less cruel than many another published this year. Among other of Nast's drawings in the campaign are one picturing Greeley nominating himself; one showing "Diogenes Greeley and Honest Tweed"; one, "Anything, Oh Anything," which presents Greeley shaking hands with John Wilkes Booth; and perhaps best known of all, "Let Us Clasp Hands Over the Bloody Chasm," which shows Greeley fraternizing with a ruffian of the South, who stands over the body of the 6th Massachusetts regiment. Nast was unrelenting in laying bare every weakness in the policies, connections, and even personal appearance of the candidate; so that the attacks sometimes awakened sympathy rather than condemnation. When the campaign closed Greeley remarked that he had doubted whether he was running for the Presidency or the penitentiary. His tragic insanity and death imediately after his defeat must have made Nast and other assailants wince to recall how unsparingly they had struck.

The anti-Grant cartoons generally lacked the force of the Republican ones; that is true even of those which Matt Morgan, coming here with a British reputation, did for *Frank Leslie's*.

THE APPLE OF DISCORD AT THE GENEVA TRIBUNAL

BY THOMAS NAST
[1872]

THE RULERS OF EUROPE look on as John Bull disposes of the Alabama Claims by consenting to a peaceful arbitration with the United States; the dispute being amicably settled when that issue has been riddled by an arrow labelled $15,500,000—the sum paid by Great Britain in settlement of American demands. At one time it had seemed possible that the claims for damage wrought during the Civil War by the British-built cruiser *Alabama* might lead to very grave difficulties. Some had even talked of war. Charles Sumner, as chairman of the Senate Foreign Relations Committee, tried to inflate the American bill to enormous dimensions. He made a speech which estimated the total damage to American interests by British infractions of neutrality at not less than $2,115,000,000; implying that the bill might be settled by the cession of the Canadian provinces to the United States. Fortunately, more temperate and reasonable counsels prevailed. The Secretary of State, Hamilton Fish, arranged for the meeting of joint commissioners from the two countries, who drew up the Treaty of Washington. Under the provisions of this compact, a whole series of troublesome questions between Great Britain and the United States was put in train for settlement. A dispute as to the boundary between British Columbia and the State of Washington, for example, was submitted to the German Emperor for adjudication. The *Alabama* claims were laid before a tribunal of five men who met in Geneva in 1872. These five are here seen sitting on the bench against the fence—Charles Francis Adams of the United States, Sir Alexander Cockburn of Great Britain, Jacques Staempfli of Switzerland, d'Itajubá of Brazil, and Count Sclopis of Italy. When the tribunal successfully completed its work, Europe and the world thrilled to the news of the first really great international arbitration of modern times: in its momentous implications, the greatest ever yet seen. From that time Anglo-American relations, which could hardly have been worse in 1870, steadily improved until between 1900 and 1914 a virtual entente was established between the two Powers.

With Nast, as we saw, a new force had entered into our political caricature. In his earlier, and best, work he showed a vigor, a directness, a power of summarizing a situation, for which we had no precedent in this country. The corrective impulse was strong in him; he apparently had a burning zeal to right the wrong. He was, said A. B. Paine, "primarily and before all a moralist." It has been said of him that he did not mirror public opinion, but led it.

A PICTURE FOR OUR EMPLOYERS
BY JOSEPH KEPPLER
[1878]

About 1870, Labor began to enter into the cartoon. In this drawing, published in *Puck*, Keppler lends effective aid to the demand for a Chinese exclusion law. Chinese laborers had begun coming to California in considerable numbers in the gold rush days of 1849. The opportunity to earn fabulous sums of money as diggers, day-laborers, and laundrymen brought them in thousands, practically all being men, because Chinese *mores* forbade a virtuous woman to emigrate. During thirty years of unrestricted immigration about three hundred thousand Chinese found homes in the United States. Large gangs of them helped build the westernmost section of the Central Pacific Railroad. Most of the immigrants were peasants from the country about Canton, of a fine type—honest, healthy, self-respecting, frugal. They did much to build the Far West, and in their gentleness, patience and dignity did not compare unfavorably with the motley white stocks that flowed into early California. But as the population on the Pacific Coast increased, the rougher white element felt increasing jealousy of all alien breeds—"greasers" from Mexico, other Latin-Americans, and the Chinese. This antagonism was not without some reasonable foundation. The Chinese were willing to toil protracted hours upon a pittance which would not support the Yankee or the Irishman. They wore clothes, occupied houses, and ate food which were below the standards demanded by white people. They refused in general to become Americanized; living as an alien race in the midst of an American civilization, they retained their ancestral language, religion, and customs. They banded together in various organizations, notably the Six Companies, which were innocent fraternal and benevolent bodies, but which naturally excited suspicion. Moreover, it became plain that if no check were interposed, California might easily become swamped by its Oriental inhabitants. There were hundreds of millions of Chinese just beyond the Pacific; steamship fares were low; inducements and facilities for migration were becoming greater. It is not strange that California raised the cry "The Chinese must go." The lurid agitator Dennis Kearney organized a workingman's party, and 1877 witnessed anti-Chinese rioting in San Francisco.

This cartoon was evoked by a more sober movement in labor circles, East as well as West, for restricting Chinese immigration to safe limits. So strong did this movement become that President Hayes in 1880 appointed a commission under President James B. Angell of the University of Michigan to negotiate a new treaty with China which would permit of regulation or suspension. The treaty was ratified the same year; in 1882 a ten-year restriction bill became law. Chinese laborers were barred from the United States, but merchants, students, or travelers were admitted on certificate.

WELCOME TO ALL!

BY JOSEPH KEPPLER
[1880]

Himself an immigrant, Keppler could execute this heartwarming cartoon with gusto. Immigration had fallen off during the long depression 1873–1878—there was no demand for workers. Now it was rising again. In the decade of the eighties, well over five million newcomers were to enter the United States. Of these nearly one-fifth would be of the "new immigration" from Eastern and Southern Europe. America, with many sparsely settled areas of great fertility, could still afford to be a land of refuge. Keppler has portrayed various national types with skill in this *Puck* cartoon of April 28, 1880. He dealt more than once with this topic. In a cartoon in *Puck* for January 11, 1893, called "Looking Backward," he amusingly showed the descendants of earlier immigrants, now more or less Americanized, holding off a new body of aliens, who with their foreign garb and manner apparently remind their forerunners too much of an ancestry which they would like to forget. In "Uncle Sam's Lodging House" (*Puck*, June 7, 1882) he pictured immigrants of various national stocks sleeping peacefully side by side—all except the Irishman, who is kicking up a shindy. In "A Picture for Employers," as we have seen, he dealt with the Chinese problem in our country, to which he returned, in a spirit of droll humor, on March 17, 1880. Here the Chinese are driven out of San Francisco and have gone to New York, where "help wanted" opens a way for them. They are taking the places of policemen, car conductors and Irish servant girls in this cartoon of "The Chinese Invasion." However, Dennis Kearney and the anti-Chinese riots in San Francisco received some serious consideration in *Puck* in 1879–1880. On May 17, 1882, appeared Gillam's "A Sop to Cerberus"; President Arthur aims at the "Western Hoodlum Vote" with a "bill excluding Chinese for ten years."

Behind the present picture of Uncle Sam as a genial host there rise various implications, suggested facts. Obviously this matter of immigration forms an interesting phase of our country's political and social development.

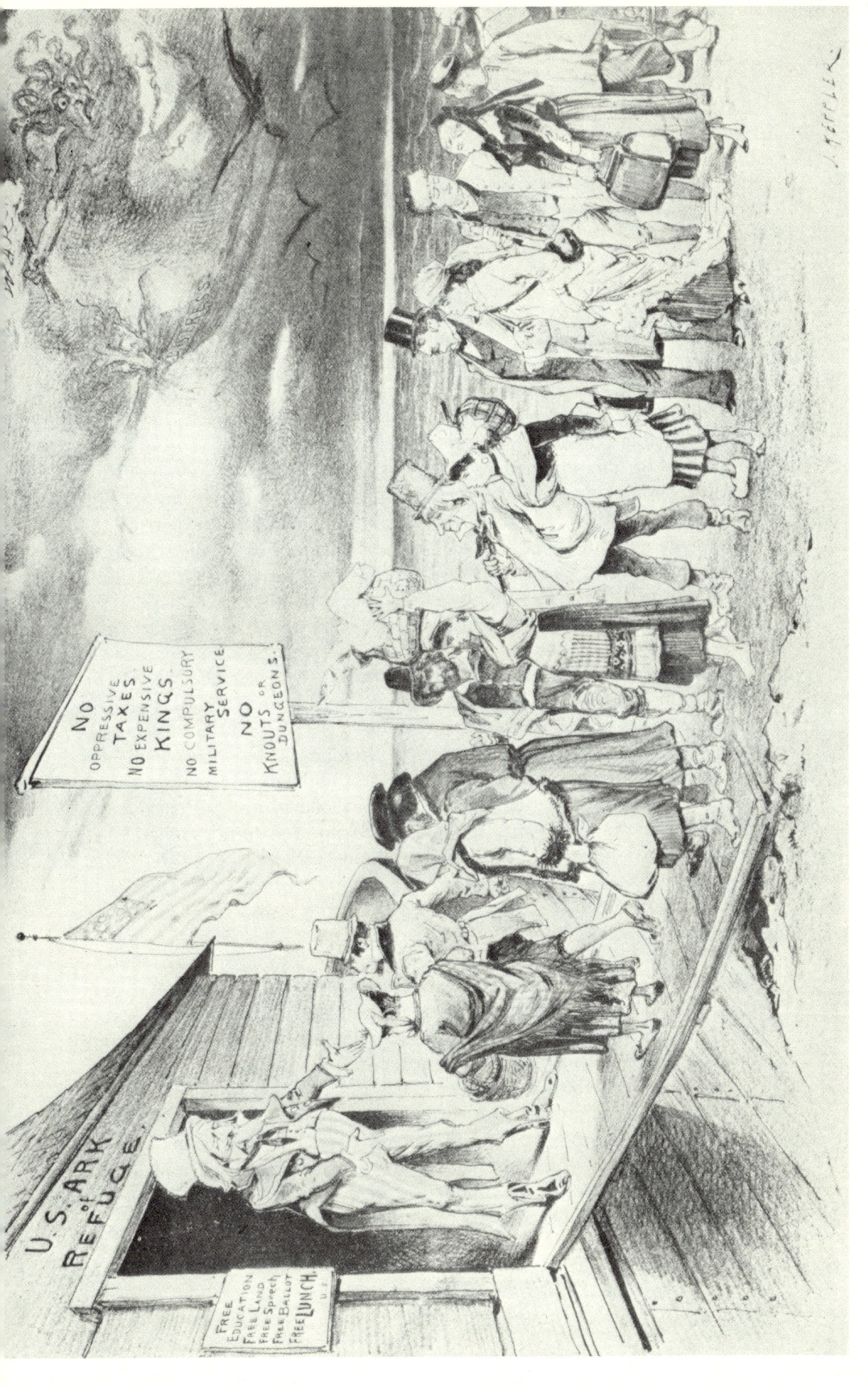

PUCK WANTS "A STRONG MAN AT THE HEAD OF GOVERNMENT"—BUT NOT THIS KIND

BY JOSEPH KEPPLER

[1880]

THE SCANDALS of the Grant Administration shocked the nation—but it was a shock from which the great mass of Republican voters rapidly recovered. As Grant was one of the poorest presidents the country has ever had, it seems almost incredible that in 1880 he was vigorously boomed for a third term; but such was the fact. Part of the explanation lies in his inextinguishable popularity with the veterans of the war; part of it in the eagerness of certain powerful State bosses, notably Roscoe Conkling of New York, Cameron of Pennsylvania, and John A. Logan of Illinois, to get him into the White House and there make use of him. A further part of the explanation, no doubt, can be found in the confidence of business interests that Grant would be not merely "safe" but pliable. At any rate, Grant had no sooner returned from his well-advertised tour around the world than the boom developed with startling suddenness and power. It was important to recall the scandals to the voters, and in the issue of *Puck* for February 4, 1880, Keppler did it. Grant hangs by the Whiskey Ring and the Navy Ring, both of which had been noisomely famous. He holds up W. W. Belknap, who as Secretary of War had taken graft from men appointed to Indian post-traderships; George M. Robeson, who as Secretary of the Navy had inexplicably become rich, and who could not or did not explain some very mysterious financial transactions with a firm that had profited enormously from naval contracts; George H. Williams, who as Attorney-General had paid household bills from departmental funds and had committed other derelictions; "Boss" Alexander R. Shepard, reputed head of a District of Columbia ring which had drawn huge profits from contracts for public improvements; Thomas Murphy, whose activities as Collector of the Port of New York had been marked by the grossest use of political spoils and by general corruption; and Orville E. Babcock, who while Grant's secretary and confidant in the White House had been one of the key figures in the Whiskey Ring, and had been indicted and tried—escaping punishment largely through Grant's influence in his behalf. The cartoon tells its story well.

Grant and his third term boom got much attention from *Puck* during this year, always unfavorable. A cartoon by Keppler in the issue of March 10, for example, entitled "An Unexpected Blow," showed Conkling and Cameron trying to fly a Grant Third Term kite, when a blast from Public Opinion wrecked it. And in "Appomattox of the Third Termers" (June 16), also by Keppler, Grant surrenders to Garfield.

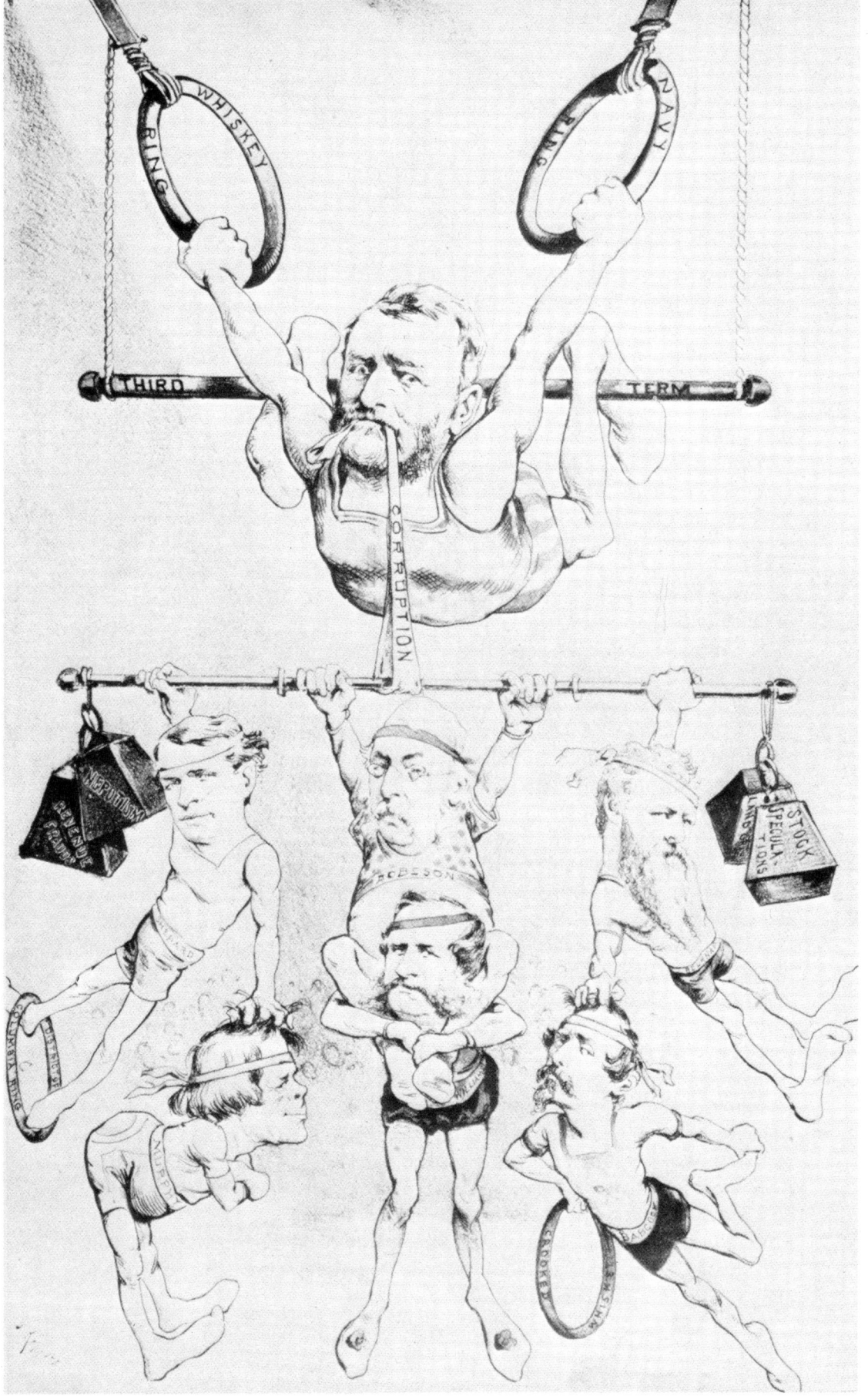

"STRONG" GOVERNMENT 1869–1877
"WEAK" GOVERNMENT 1877–1880

BY JAMES A. WALES

[1880]

"RECONSTRUCTION" ENDED when on April 10, 1877, President Hayes withdrew the last Federal troops from South Carolina, and on April 24, 1877, removed the last detachments from New Orleans. This was in pursuance of what was called "the bargain"—an agreement between Republican and Democratic leaders that, if the Democrats would acquiesce in Hayes's inauguration, he would put a final end to national interference in the South. Even without the bargain, he would have had no choice. It had become plain that Southern whites would no longer tolerate bayonet rule, and even Southern Negroes were tired of an artificial and unworkable system. No sooner was the sectional controversy ended than Southern progress found a new impetus. A New South emerged from the wreckage of the old regime, a South where agriculture became more diversified, with attention to cereals, fruits, nuts, and vegetables as well as cotton, sugar, and tobacco; a South where textile factories, coal mines, iron mills, and furniture establishments created numerous centers of industrialism. By 1900 the South had almost half of the total number of cotton mills in the nation. For a time the Stalwart supporters of Grant, along with a few surviving Abolitionists of the Garrison-Wendell Phillips type, loudly lamented the "abandonment" of the Southern Negro and the reëstablishment of white supremacy. The Abolitionists had a humanitarian motive, or believed they had; the Stalwarts regretted the loss of Republican Congressmen and Presidential electors from the old Carpetbag areas. But the vast majority of Americans recognized that the counter-revolution in the South was wholesome and inevitable. Here the cartoonist, by a contrast between the sad years of Federal intervention and the brighter new era, deals a shrewd blow at the Stalwarts and pays a deserved tribute to Rutherford B. Hayes. That rather colorless President never impressed the American imagination; but he was honest and liberal, and he performed a national service in helping to plow under the bloody shirt and the musket.

James Albert Wales's best cartooning was done for *Puck* and *Judge* between 1877 and 1886. He had not the slashing power of Nast and was less imaginative than Keppler; but at his best he did good work, and he had a special gift for portraiture. It is to be noted that Keppler also dealt appreciatively with President Hayes. For example, in "Erl King," published in *Puck* October 31, 1877, he showed Hayes riding fearlessly through a dark and terrible night with the infant Civil Service Reform in his arms. The present cartoon by Wales appeared in *Puck* of May 12, 1880, when a new Presidential campaign was about to revive the discussion of Reconstruction.

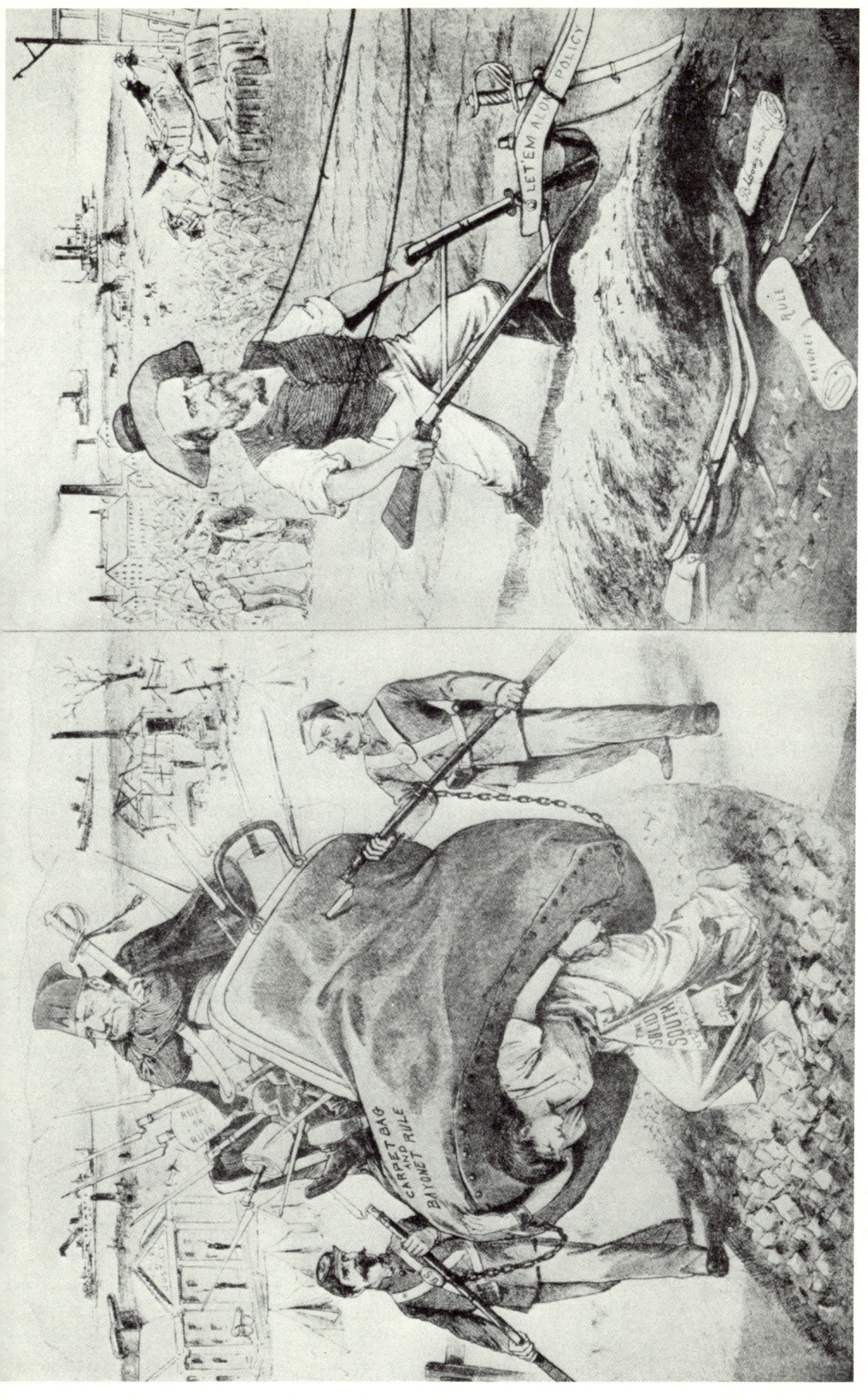

FORBIDDING THE BANNS

BY JOSEPH KEPPLER

[1880]

ONCE JAMES A. GARFIELD had been nominated by the Republicans in 1880, the question whether he could be elected seemed to many doubtful. The Stalwart wing of the party sulked for weeks, and waited for a promise that if seated in the White House, Garfield would "recognize" them by suitable grants of patronage. Much argument and cajolery had to be expended upon the proud Roscoe Conkling. It was not until September that he, with Cameron and Grant, decided to give open support to the ticket. Conkling made a speechmaking tour, and spoke at a meeting in Garfield's old Ohio district over which Grant presided; even so, many Stalwarts remained disgusted. Moreover, Garfield's political past was not proof against criticism. He had been implicated by Oakes Ames in the Credit Mobilier scandal—Ames having distributed stock of the highly profitable Credit Mobilier Company to members of Congress in order, it was believed, to purchase their acquiescence in the method by which that corporation was used to make huge profits out of the construction of the Union Pacific Railroad. Garfield always denied that he really was implicated; his name was down in Ames's memorandum book, but he declared that Ames did not remember the true nature of their business relations, and that he was quite innocent. The voters of his Congressional district had accepted this view at the time, and cordially reëlected him. Yet the charge rose up to plague him throughout his political career. Here William H. Barnum, the Democratic National Chairman, is shown reviving it—to the consternation of the rigidly virtuous Carl Schurz and prim Whitelaw Reid. Conkling and Logan, whispering in the background, evidently take a more cynical attitude. The bride, Garfield, says: "But it was such a little one." The sum involved was $329.

For present-day taste the cartoon is audacious, to say the least, but the eighties had a stronger stomach in political affairs. Moreover, the breezy humor of the drawing, its vigor and point, remove or rather bury out of sight the coarseness of the underlying idea. Keppler makes his satire understood with a directness that carries all before it; his audacity is a means, not an end. So effective is the cartoon that we can readily imagine Republicans as well as Democrats chuckling over it.

In "The Army Worm" (July 7, 1880), Keppler shows Garfield in a long parade of Army worms with heads of generals, stopped by the rock "Credit Mobilier." In "Just the Difference" (July 28, 1880) Hancock, the Democratic candidate, carries his party, while Garfield is carried by his. But when Garfield had reached the White House Keppler depicts him in "The American Sixtus V" (May 18, 1881) as the Pope throwing away the crutches "Conciliation" and "Weakness."

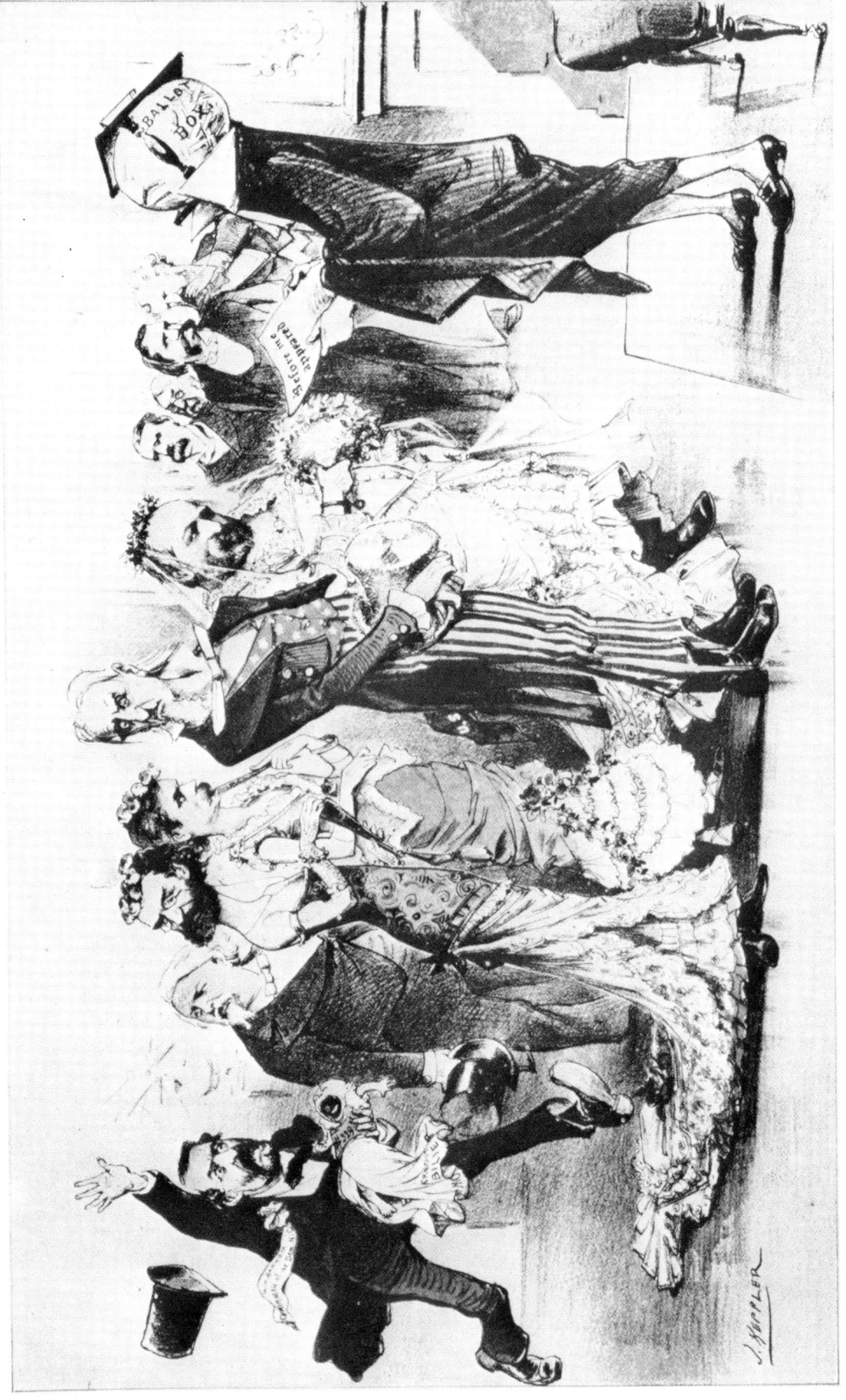

THE CINDERELLA OF THE REPUBLICAN PARTY AND HER HAUGHTY SISTERS

BY JOSEPH KEPPLER
[1880]

THIS CARTOON OFFERS an apt summing-up of the Hayes Administration, full of liberal and constructive effort, but somehow disdained by a country that fixed attention on less worthy leaders. Cinderella Hayes, watching his "Prosperity Soup," sits forlorn and unregarded in his shining kitchen. The shelves are full of evidences of his good works. Among the jars and bottles are "Fair Southern Policy"—he had let the South take care of its own affairs; "Silver Bill Veto"—he had unavailingly tried to kill the Bland-Allison Bill, which provided for a dangerously heavy coinage of silver dollars, to be full legal tender; "Resumption Jam"—specie payments had been resumed on January 1, 1879; "Potted Corruption"—Hayes had done much to clean up the last vestiges of the dishonesty rampant in the Grant Administration; "Chinese Bill Veto"—he had vetoed an exclusion bill which flagrantly violated the existing treaty with China, and had taken steps to get a new and better treaty; and "Civil Service Reform"—he had been an earnest friend of that great cause. Hayes, who possessed many fine qualities, would have left a stronger impression on the nation had he not entered office under the cloud of the disputed election, and had he not made the error of announcing that he would serve only one term. The Stalwart wing of the Republican Party never liked him, and the country paid much more attention to the vain, imperious, rhetorical Roscoe Conkling—every speech his "greatest effort"—and to Grant, beribboned with the ovations received on his tour of the world.

This is a notable example of Keppler's power in rendering facial expression. In 1876–77 *Puck* appeared in New York; from that moment Nast had a worthy rival. Keppler, an Austrian by birth, had a vein of Viennese gaiety and a grace of artistic approach which tempered his satire, and made it all the more subtly effective. He was always lightfooted; his weapon was the rapier, not the club. He showed an artist's instinct, giving careful attention to composition, and introducing landscapes whenever possible. Like Nast, he often drew upon the great masters of letters for symbols and themes. Although his Austrian characteristics remained evident throughout his life, he grew increasingly expert in presenting the spirit and significance of the American scene. His work offers another forcible proof that caricature has a wide range, and that no one word—caricature, cartooning, comic art—is quite adequate to describe all that is implied in the drawings of such men as Gillray, Daumier, Keppler, Nast, Gillam, and J. N. Darling. On the staff of *Puck* Keppler gathered an array of able artists, among them J. A. Wales, Bernhard Gillam, F. B. Opper, Louis Dalrymple, E. Zimmerman.

A HARMLESS EXPLOSION

BY JOSEPH KEPPLER
[1881]

FEW EPISODES in American politics had the opera bouffe quality of Roscoe Conkling's famous resignation from the Senate on May 18, 1881, in a fit of political pique—a resignation which amounted to political suicide. But the episode had a tragic sequel, for Guiteau's assassination of President Garfield grew in part out of the hostility between Stalwart Republicans and Half-Breed Republicans which had led to Conkling's step. The proud, imperious Conkling, with real ability under his colossal conceit, had been Senator from New York since 1867. During the Grant Administration he was one of the simple-minded President's most potent lieutenants, and controlled dispensation of offices and contracts in New York with iron hand. His friend and henchman Chester A. Arthur was made head of the New York Custom House. When Hayes was elected President on a reform platform, Conkling was filled with disgust and indignation. He waged ceaseless war against Hayes and the Half-Breeds. Tightening his grip on the New York machine, he did his utmost in 1880 to force the renomination of Grant for a third term. Failure in this left him disgruntled, and he watched the new President, Garfield, with suspicious eye. Garfield tried to divide offices fairly between Stalwarts and Half-Breeds; he nominated some of Conkling's best friends to important places; then, to keep the balance true, he named Conkling's chief enemy in New York to the headship of the Custom House, a key position in political affairs. Stung to fury, Conkling tried for a time to defeat the nomination in the Senate. When he saw that he was to be beaten, he and Tom Platt, the junior Senator, resigned their seats to appeal to the New York legislature. They believed it would sustain them and send them back to Washington. Instead, it sustained Garfield, and chose new Senators who would support the President. The blow was crushing to Conkling's pride, and finished his political career. Turning to legal practice, he never again sought office. But when Guiteau shot Garfield in July, it was with the exclamation: "I am a Stalwart, and now Chester A. Arthur is President."

This wonderful caricature, full of hilarity, portrays the final disruption of the great American windbag, with "Me Too" Platt (who as a matter of fact had taken the initiative in the resignations) as a collapsing appendage. The same event was treated with equally cutting satire by Nast, in "Plucked of his Plumage (or Patronage) the Jackdaw is again nothing but a Jackdaw" (*Harper's Weekly*, August 6, 1881), the plumage representing various offices. Conkling's strutting pose was often presented by Keppler, changing moods being indicated with subtle exaggerations that emphasized the point intended.

A GRAND SHAKESPEREAN REVIVAL

BY JOSEPH KEPPLER

[1881]

Seldom has shakespeare been quoted more aptly. Chester A. Arthur's accession to power was as sudden as Prince Hal's; he bore the same reputation (politically) for loose living and good fellowship. Conkling's expectations of preferment were as keen as Falstaff's had been. Had not he been Arthur's bosom associate, guide and mentor, in the State machine? When President Hayes ejected Arthur from the New York Custom House, Conkling had made the Senate ring with defense of his friend and pupil. The nomination of Garfield in 1880 was such a heavy blow to the Stalwart Republicans that Arthur was picked for the Vice Presidency to conciliate them. Now Guiteau's bullet made him President, and the Stalwarts, from ex-president Grant down to such minor, ill-regarded politicians as Tom Platt of New York, T. W. Brady of Indiana, and Stephen W. Dorsey of Arkansas (the two latter the chief figures in the Star Route frauds), all rejoiced. Their jubilation was premature. In this cartoon Keppler included a cautionary subtitle—he had little hope of seeing Arthur play Prince Hal's dignified and public-spirited role. Yet this is precisely what Arthur did. Realizing to the full the obligations of his new position, he turned a cold shoulder to his old associates in politics, made appointments with careful regard to fitness, and gave his Administration an admirable dignity and decorum. He signed some excellent legislation, showed courage in vetoing a bad rivers and harbors bill, and left office high in the regard of the nation. Conkling, who had resigned from the Senate in a huff after quarreling with Garfield, might have taken a seat on the Supreme Court bench from Arthur; but he refused it and remained in private employment as a highly paid corporation attorney.

This is a particularly good example of the cartoon carrying an allusion to literature or mythology, far commoner then than now. It is also an excellent specimen of Keppler's skill. The story of King Arthur's rejection of Conkling-Falstaff is beautifully presented, and despite the many figures, presented very clearly. The lesser personages are grouped around Arthur and Conkling so as to emphasize the point. The facial expression, too, is well handled—particularly with Conkling and Platt. Keppler might well have plumed himself on his prophetic powers, for this cartoon appeared in *Puck* on October 5, 1881, before Arthur had had time to develop his attitude. Another Shakespearean cartoon of similar character, by Gillam, in *Puck* of December 28, 1881, entitled "The Path of Duty," showed Arthur as Hamlet preparing to follow the ghost of Garfield; the latter holding up a scroll which exhorts the new President to prosecute the Star Route cases.

A GRAND SHAKESPERIAN REVIVAL
Which We Have But Little Hope of Seeing on the Stage of the National Capital

THE MODERN PROMETHEUS
BY BERNHARD GILLAM
[1882]

Here is one of the first shots in the long battle against pools, trusts, holding companies, and other forms of big-business consolidation; a battle still far from ended. When it appeared the word "trust" was not yet known in this connection, or Gillam would doubtless have used it. But pools, mergers, and other combinations had become numerous and powerful enough to frighten many Americans. The dislike of monopoly could be traced in English-speaking lands back to Tudor England, and the common law attack on monopoly runs back to that period. In the United States men had always believed in free competition, and had felt a predilection for small business units. After the Civil War an unbridled competition unfortunately had ruinous effects in various industries. Rate wars between competing railroads often ended in bankruptcy; price-slashing on the part of mining-interests, manufacturers, oil-refiners, and other businesses had the same consequence. When an Industrial Commission investigated the rise of monopolies near the end of the century, it reported that the main force behind business consolidation was "competition so vigorous that profits of nearly all competing establishments were destroyed." The railroads in the sixties and seventies formed numerous pools; so numerous, indeed, that by 1890 very few railroads were outside a pool. Pools also became popular among manufacturers. But they were illegal under the common law, and pooling contracts could therefore not be enforced in the courts. It was necessary to invent new devices. Outright consolidation was difficult. The Standard Oil Company under Rockefeller therefore in 1879–82 perfected the trust agreement, which made it easy to create an effective monopoly. It at once found imitators in lead-mining, whiskey distilling, sugar refining, tobacco manufacturing, and other fields. By 1890 the number of trusts was becoming prodigious, and the government that year aimed the Sherman Anti-Trust Act against them. The process of business consolidation proved irresistible, and on the whole beneficial. But the tyrannical excesses of the great monopolies between 1880 and 1900 aroused consternation and anger. When Gillam drew this forceful cartoon, he had before him the results of the Hepburn Investigation of 1879 into the rebating abuses of the railroads and the rise of a number of hardfisted business combinations.

Even earlier, Keppler had published in *Puck* (February 9, 1881) a cartoon "In Danger," showing Columbia faced by the huge snake Monopoly; python and octopus were subsequently frequently used as symbols of monopoly. In the next twenty years a long list of vigorous anti-monopoly cartoons were published by organs of every party; and when Theodore Roosevelt established his Bureau of Corporations and launched on a campaign of trust-busting, the cartoons were multiplied.

FIRST ANNUAL PICNIC OF THE "KNIGHTS OF LABOR"

BY JOSEPH KEPPLER

[1882]

It was in 1882 that Labor Day was suggested, and the first Labor Day Parade was held. By this time, too, the Noble Order of the Knights of Labor was coming into prominence. Founded by a Philadelphia garment-worker, Uriah S. Stevens, in 1869, it had grown slowly and at first half-secretly. It was not until 1875 that it held its first national convention. At the time this cartoon appeared its membership probably did not exceed 50,000. But new leaders were taking charge, the secret features (which had repelled Catholics) were dropped, and as prosperity returned after the long depression of 1873–79, its vigor increased. Within a few years it laid claim to a membership of over 700,000, and its head, Terence V. Powderly, was a national power. Its programme called for an eight-hour day, inheritance and income taxes, postal savings banks, government ownership of public utilities, and the development of cooperative organizations in the field of industry. For a time it seemed likely to exert great influence. But its organization (as this cartoon indicates) was defective; its membership was heterogeneous, with a very large proportion of unskilled workers; and a series of unfortunate strikes weakened it. In the later eighties it declined as rapidly as it had risen.

Keppler's strong sympathy for the workers gives the cartoon a poignant appeal. The fat capitalists—Jay Gould, Russell Sage, Cyrus W. Field, Hal Roach the shipbuilder, and William H. Vanderbilt—look on with amusement as a poor workingman climbs the slippery pole to get bread and meat for his family. The artist shows us a tub of "monopoly grease" at the foot of the pole. But the capitalists had other weapons against the worker as well; the blacklist, the "yellow dog contract," the lockout, the refusal to tolerate unions, the rejection of arbitration.

This drawing appeared on June 21, 1882, in *Puck*, the cartoons in which, like Nast's in *Harper's Weekly*, were generally friendly to labor and against union domination, the boycott, and the agitator. The advantages of arbitration were stressed, as in "Arbitration—True Balance" (*Puck*, March 17, 1886), in which Capital and Labor are meddling with the clock "Business." Naturally, Labor was also brought into the pictorial arguments for and against Protection and Free Trade, with later the "full dinner pail" as a useful symbol. Just as obviously, Labor entered into anti-monopoly cartoons. An example of the last is found in Keppler's "Passing Everything on the Road" (*Puck*, February 6, 1884), which pictures Standard Oil and other monopolies, riding behind spanking teams, leaving Labor's miserable rig well behind.

UNCLE SAM'S NEGLECTED FARM

BY JOSEPH KEPPLER

[1882]

CIVIL SERVICE REFORM had become a crying need by the beginning of the eighties, and many people believed that a new and more honest party was required. Keppler's cartoon (*Puck*, August 23, 1882) reflects the disgust and discouragement of many Americans in the year following Garfields' death at the hands of an assassin. His murder by Guiteau had grown out of the wretched squabbles between the Stalwart and Half-Breed Republicans. Chester A. Arthur, now in the White House, had had an unsavory record as a spoils politician. The Democratic Party had a bad record of Southern secession, Bourbonism, and Tammanyism; the Republican Party a bad record of Grantism, bossism, and general corruption. Why not an independent and liberal new party?—why not the merit system in the Federal civil service? The independent impulse in politics soon gave the country the Mugwumps of 1884, who refused to accept the Blaine ticket and stood for reform along a broad front. The demand for the merit system gave the country the Pendleton Act of 1883, introducing a classified civil service to which appointments were made after examination, and in which advancement was for efficient conduct. This cartoon interprets the liberal spirit of a host of public-spirited men in the period; a spirit very far from radical, but insistent upon more honesty and expertness in public affairs. The rickety Navy Department corncrib and Interior Department barn in the background represent two of the weakest spots in American administration.

The "New and Independent Party" in this cartoon asks for the job on the farm in place of "those two quarrelsome fellows," the Democrat and the Republican. The figure of this Independent Party—a handsome young man wearing a red shirt and boots—was much used by *Puck* during the Cleveland-Blaine campaign of 1884, often holding an axe presumably symbolic. What the independent vote meant to the Democrats is indicated by Keppler's cartoon "A Sail, a Sail" (*Puck*, July 2, 1884), in which Democracy, as a woman on a shore in hostile land, with John Kelly of Tammany as an Indian lurking behind her, is looking for deliverance to the ship of the Independent Republicans. In still another *Puck* drawing (December 3, 1884) the young Independent is giving blood to old man Democracy, infusing new life into him.

THE WRITING ON THE WALL
BY JOSEPH KEPPLER
[1884]

THE NOMINATION OF James G. Blaine in 1884 produced the memorable revolt of Independents or Mugwumps within the Republican Party, reaching most formidable proportions almost overnight. The nomination had hardly been announced before hundreds of prominent men declared their intention of bolting it. On June 8 the New York *Times* printed three columns of letters from indignant Republicans. Among the rebels were Carl Schurz, Henry Ward Beecher, George Haven Putnam, Charles Francis Adams, Jr., Benjamin H. Bristow, Charles W. Eliot, James Russell Lowell, Richard H. Dana, Josiah Quincy, and Thomas Wentworth Higginson. One Republican newspaper after another went over to support Blaine's opponent, Grover Cleveland. Among these were the *Nation, Harper's Weekly,* the New York *Times, Herald,* and *Evening Post,* and the Boston *Transcript* and *Herald.* All dissenting men and journals took the view that Blaine's political record was so tainted with demagogy and corruption that his election would be a disaster. Their opinion was fortified when a new batch of the so-called Mulligan letters, throwing light upon Blaine's allegedly improper connection with the Little Rock & Fort Smith Railroad, and allegedly improper sale of Union Pacific bonds, was published. The Republicans, bitter over these attacks, exploited to the utmost some accusations against Cleveland founded upon an old Buffalo story regarding his private life. This had little effect. Prominent ministers, including James Freeman Clarke, after careful investigation, took their stand behind Cleveland.

Puck was one of the journals which swung to Cleveland, and with Keppler, Gillam, and other artists, it did effective work for the Democratic ticket. On June 18, 1884, appeared this spirited drawing of tattooed Blaine and his supporters thrown into confusion by the handwriting on the wall. Keppler delighted in such compositions, showing many figures in agitated attitudes. He had first used the tattooing idea in a cartoon of 1876, showing Columbia stained all over with letters reading "Whiskey Ring," "Black Friday," "Credit Mobilier," and the like. Bernhard Gillam had represented Blaine as hideously tattooed in a cartoon in *Puck* for April 16, 1884, entitled "National Dime Museum." The weekly continued to depict him as thus ineffaceably marked with his discreditable past. Its most daring picture was "Phryne before the Chicago Tribunal," an adaptation of J. L. Gérôme's painting; Phryne-Blaine was being unveiled to the gaze of the Republican leaders at the Chicago Convention by Whitelaw Reid. But the theme was sometimes abandoned for another. In "The False Friend of the Workingman" (*Puck*, October 15, 1884) Keppler presented Blaine in formal garb, with high hat and frock coat, in elegant contrast to the hungry miners of the Hocking Valley, thrown out of work by imported Italian labor.

THE BLAINE TARIFF FRAUD

BY THOMAS NAST
[1884]

THE BITTERNESS of this presidential contest produced many vulgar and unfair cartoons on both sides. But Nast did not hit below the belt in his depiction of the "plumed knight" masquerading as a friend of the workingman. The egregious Ben Butler was running for President on the Anti-Monopoly and Greenback tickets, with a platform with demagogic appeals to labor. Men had ceased to believe in Butler's sincerity; first Democrat, then Radical Republican, then Democrat again, and now a nondescript, he was always playing some sly game. The general assumption was that he intended to draw labor votes away from Cleveland, and thus benefit Blaine. If this were true, he failed, for he polled only 175,000 votes. A poster at the back calls attention to the fact that Dana of the *Sun* made the blunder of supporting Butler's absurd candidacy. Appearing in *Harper's Weekly* on November 1st, this cartoon was one of Nast's final thrusts at Blaine.

HE CAN'T BEAT HIS OWN RECORD

BY JOSEPH KEPPLER
[1884]

NOR WAS THERE ANYTHING unjust in this earlier cartoon (*Puck*, July 30), which offered a Mugwump explanation of the reasons why Blaine could not win. His record of demagogy, bluster, friendship with monopolists, and railroad scandal, according to his enemies, must defeat him. The words "guano statesmanship" on the tattooed man allude to his dealings, while Secretary of State, with Chile and Peru. Although this cartoon appeared in midsummer, Jay Gould, Cyrus W. Field, and Russell Sage were all in evidence. They became much more prominent when, just before election day, Blaine was a guest at the famous millionaires' dinner, or "Feast of Belshazzar," as it was called in Walt McDougall's cartoon in the New York *World*. Note also that Whitelaw Reid as bucket-holder, with the *Tribune* as sponge, wears a very unhappy expression. Mugwump cartoonists were able to publish I-told-you-so drawings after the election. Keppler's was especially happy. Called "Men may come and Men may go, but the Work of Reform shall go on forever," it showed George William Curtis, Henry Ward Beecher, James Freeman Clarke, and other idealists of the period working on the great permanent structure of reform.

FOES IN HIS PATH. THE HERCULEAN TASK BEFORE OUR NEXT PRESIDENT

BY BERNHARD GILLAM

[1885]

To A LATER and more heavily troubled generation, the tasks of Cleveland's first Administration, 1885–89, do not seem to have been formidable. But to Americans of the time they looked difficult enough; and with a divided Congress (the Senate being Republican) and a conservative idea of Presidential leadership, Cleveland found progress difficult. He attacked all the problems here indicated with stubborn courage. Spoils politicians were discomfited by honest execution of the civil service laws and steady extension of the merit system. Land-grabbers were routed by government action, that is, railroad corporations which had failed to earn the huge land-grants given them under certain stipulations were compelled to disgorge tens of millions of acres, while cattle-ranchers were driven off Indian reservations and frauds in the Land Office were stopped. The "rotten navy," management of which had more than once been castigated by *Puck*, was put on its feet by Cleveland's brilliant Secretary of the Navy, William C. Whitney. Excessive silver coinage under the Bland-Allison Act was denounced by the President, and though it could not be stopped, a basis was laid for his subsequent battle against the free and unlimited coinage of silver. The high tariff was assailed, and although the Republican Senate halted all attempts at a downward revision, Cleveland made the question the central issue of the campaign of 1888, and awakened the country to its far-reaching importance. Altogether, he gave the United States the best Administration it had had since the Civil War. His presentation in the role of Hercules is quaint enough, but it had a certain aptitude. There is a foreshadowing of all this reform spirit in a cartoon by Nast, published in *Harper's Weekly* of April 19, 1884, while Cleveland was still governor of New York. Entitled "Reform without Bloodshed," it pictures him seated, with young Theodore Roosevelt standing beside him, working out reform for New York City.

The present cartoon, published in *Puck* on February 18, was one of the last in which Gillam treated Cleveland in a complimentary spirit, for he went in 1886 to *Judge*, and as chief artist and part owner of that comic weekly he consistently took the anti-Democratic side. Like some others of our best cartoonists, Gillam was foreign-born, an Englishman brought to America as a boy. His work, especially his earlier line drawings, showed a severity of manner that recalled Tenniel. Like Nast and Keppler he drew freely on literature for allusions, knew American politics, and had a keen sense of wit.

NO WELCOME FOR THE LITTLE STRANGER
BY EUGENE ZIMMERMAN
[1885]

WHEN CLEVELAND made it plain that in his appointments he would support the spirit as well as the letter of the Pendleton Civil Service Act of 1883, a party storm broke around his head. For the first time since Buchanan left the White House, a Democrat was in a position to reward loyal adherents with national offices—and Cleveland thought more about merit than services. Six months passed, and still only ten or twelve per cent of the Federal positions were occupied by Democrats. Naturally the older leaders and machine workers felt outraged. "Cleveland must remember," asserted Pulitzer's *World*, "the obligations which an Administration elected by a great historical party owes to that party." Senator Eustis, head of a political ring in Louisiana, was still more emphatic. When Cleveland appointed honest and efficient men to the custom house and post office in New Orleans, ignoring the State machine, Eustis roared with rage. He branded Cleveland as a "conspicuous and humiliating failure," guilty of "treacherous conduct toward the party he claims to represent," and threatened that if he did not reward the faithful with more government plums, he and his Cabinet "shall fall and be buried in the ruins they have made." Fortunately, Cleveland stood by his principles. Republicans who had proved incompetent or who were guilty of "pernicious partisanship" were removed; others were in large part replaced after they had served four full years. But there were no sweeping changes for spoils purposes. Zimmerman shows the President protecting the Civil Service Reform baby while Pulitzer, Charles A. Dana, Eustis, Governor David B. Hill of New York, Thomas A. Hendricks of Indiana, and others annoy it to the top of their bent.

As early as March of this same year 1885, *Puck* published Gillam's "Good Samaritan," with Cleveland aiding Civil Service, whom Hayes and Garfield have passed by (rather unfair to Hayes). In December, Keppler's "Carol of the Waits" depicted the "outs," including Pulitzer, singing in the snow outside the President's window. Again, on March 2, 1887, Lohengrin Cleveland is protecting the Democratic Elsa from Ortrud Pulitzer, Telramund Hill, and the band of "Jacksonian Bourbons" and "Heelers." Indeed, *Puck* from the beginning of its career fought for the cause of Civil Service Reform, sometimes referred to by its opponents as "Snivel Service Reform."

Zimmerman, when this drawing appeared in *Puck* on October 21, was evidently much under the influence of Keppler, whose manner he caught to some extent. But he already showed intimations of the grotesquerie which he later, particularly in his work for *Judge*, made highly effective over the signature "Zim."

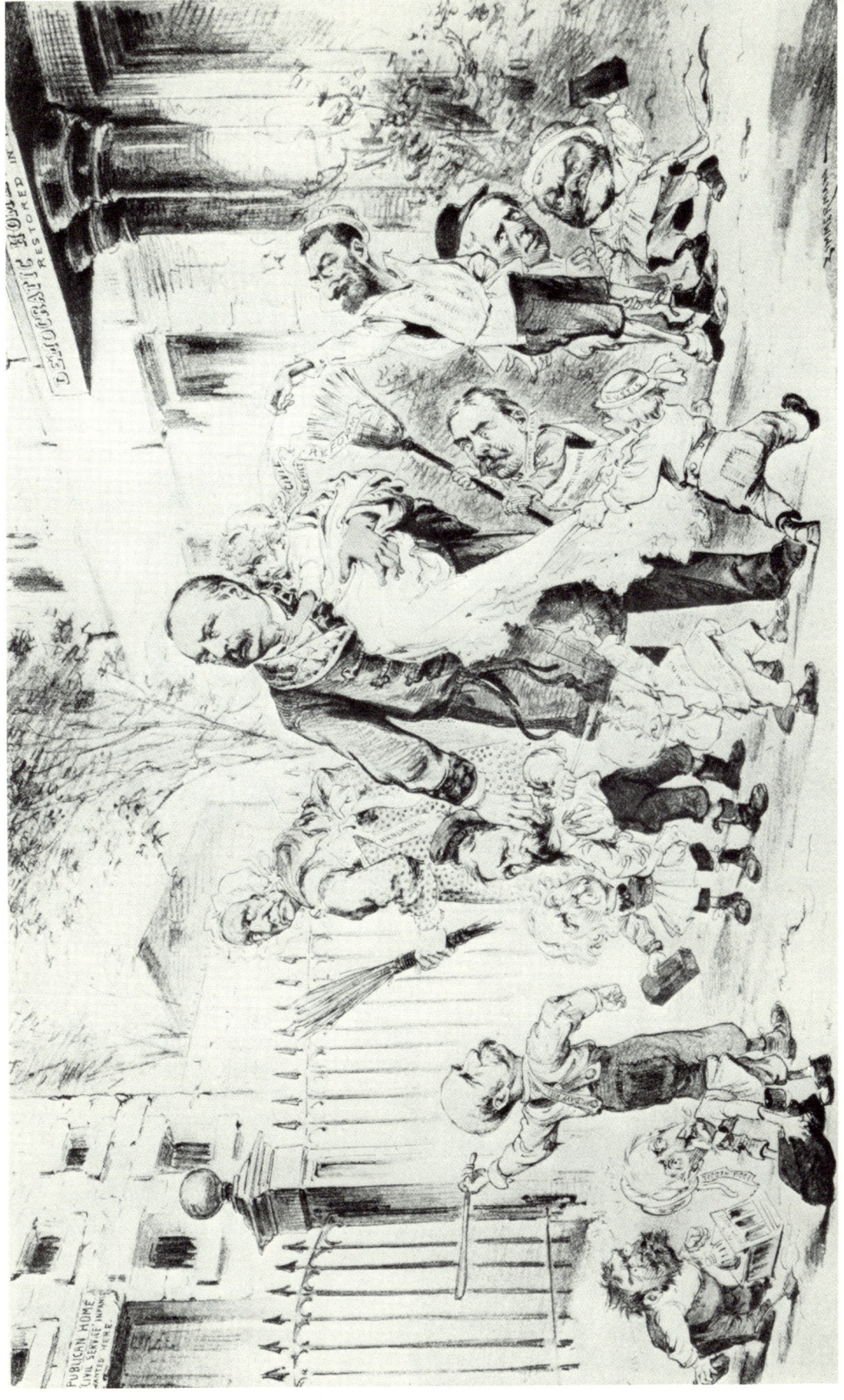

THE FREE-TRADE BUGABOO
BY CHARLES J. TAYLOR
[1886]

CLEVELAND'S ELECTION gave liberal men hope, for the first time in many years, that a reduction of the tariff might soon be possible, and it caused the advocates of high protection to redouble their efforts in its behalf. Such men as James M. Swank, secretary of the American Iron and Steel Association, harped upon the theme that lower duties would mean competition of European "pauper" labor, and a fall in wages. In 1886–87 Swank distributed high-tariff pamphlets by the million, chiefly among workingmen and farmers. Taylor ridicules the bugaboo, but admits that it was having some effect. The fact was that neither farmers nor laborers quite saw their true interest in tariff reform. Not until 1892, when the Homestead Massacre advertised the fact that the highly protected iron and steel mills of Andrew Carnegie were treating labor badly and paying low wages while making egregiously high profits, did workingmen vote in large numbers for a low-tariff candidate. Taylor exhibits an employer who pays sixty-two cents for a twelve-hour day. This was an exaggeration, but dollar wages for a ten- or eleven-hour day were common.

Taylor, an illustrator of society rather than politics, did his share of political cartoons for *Puck*. His comment on the tariff has refreshing originality and plentiful truth. Other cartoonists, in dealing with the subject, played up the full dinner pail or pictured the very overgrown infant industry. One of the best hits was "The Original Coxey's Army," by W. A. Rogers, in *Harper's Weekly* of May 12, 1894; Carnegie and other very prosperous manufacturers marching on Washington under the banner "Feed our Infant Industries." Another memorable drawing was "Tedlet's Soliloquy," by Joseph Keppler, Jr., in *Puck*, October 30, 1907. It has only one figure, Theodore Roosevelt, seated in the traditional curule chair of actors of Hamlet, wearing a troubled air and quoting: "Thus the *Tariff* does make cowards of us all." The artist had hit upon a significant fact in party history and in T. R.'s career.

Labor was continually admonished, by each side, to realize where its salvation lay—"Codlin's the friend, not Short," in the language of Dickens's "Old Curiosity Shop." In Keppler's "A Parallel from Fiction" (*Puck*, May 9, 1888) Labor plays the part of the emperor in Hans Christian Andersen's story "The Emperor's New Clothes." Kelley, Randall and others in the parade strive to persuade the public that the paper-capped workman in underclothes is wearing "magnificent garments" furnished by "Protection." *Puck*, speaking to a group of perplexed workmen, presumably takes the part of the little child in the story who breaks the spell by saying: "But he has nothing on."

THE REAL STRUGGLE.
THE TRUE AND THE FALSE FRIENDS
OF THE WORKING-MAN

BY JOSEPH KEPPLER

[1886]

HERE WE HAVE *Puck's* response, May 12, 1886, to the Haymarket Riot which had occurred in Chicago eight days earlier, and to the other labor violence of this spring. On the night of May 4 a crowd of about 1300 men had gathered in Haymarket Square to listen to speeches by agitators connected with the anarchist movement. Strong feeling had been aroused among workingmen by a lockout of the employees at Cyrus McCormick's reaper works in the city, and by a widespread strike then under way in behalf of the eight-hour day. But the meeting was orderly. Just as it was closing, a platoon of police appeared to clear away the crowd; and as they marched up, a bomb from some unknown hand exploded among them, killing or fatally wounding seven policemen and injuring some forty others. The survivors fired repeated volleys into the fleeing crowd. This tragic episode sent a thrill of horror and indignation throughout the country. Friends of labor feared that its just demands were about to be discredited by the violence of a few fanatical anarchists and socialists, recruited chiefly from Europe. The fact that a great strike took place this spring on the Gould railway lines in the Southwest, causing a widespread blockade of freight west of the Mississippi, and the fact that the Knights of Labor now boasted over 700,000 members, caused the nation to take a keener interest in the labor question than ever before. Keppler shows the more responsible friends of the worker, Chief Arthur of the Brotherhood of Locomotive Engineers, and Terence V. Powderly of the Knights of Labor, assisting him through the gateway of arbitration to peace and order; while Anarchy and Violence try to drag him down into the mire of bloodshed and disorder. It is a well-conceived cartoon, which after Keppler's fashion makes good use of the effects of contrasting dark and light to heighten the dramatic impression. The cartoonist was uniformly sympathetic toward labor, hostile toward agitators. This hostility extended, when later this year Henry George ran for the mayoralty of New York against Abram S. Hewitt and Theodore Roosevelt, to some fierce attacks upon George and his single-tax ideas.

THE OPENING OF THE CONGRESSIONAL SESSION

BY JOSEPH KEPPLER

[1887]

THIS ARRESTING COMPOSITION is dominated by the huge monster "Surplus," with its tail "Tariff Question," which crowds the hall of Congress. The surplus question had come to dominate American affairs and to make the tariff issue unescapable. Keppler's cartoon was published on December 7, 1887, the day after President Cleveland had sent to Congress a message entirely devoted to the tariff, and which pointed out that "it is a condition, not a theory, that confronts us." A financial surplus might seem a rather happy condition. Actually, a large surplus is often more embarrassing than a deficit, and may even be a national calamity. The facts were fairly simple. The country in the fiscal year 1886–87 had enjoyed a revenue of something over $370,000,000. This, the national expenses being small, was about $103,000,000 more than it needed. It could not well employ the surplus in reducing the national debt, for the outstanding four per cent bonds were not callable at par till the end of the century, and if the government bought them in the open market it would have to pay a high premium. That is, it would be taking money from poor taxpayers to pour it into the pockets of wealthy bondholders. To use the surplus for public buildings, making harbors, deepening rivers, and the like, was justifiable only up to a certain point; beyond that expenditures would be sheer waste. If the money were kept in the Treasury, a dangerous shortage of currency might develop. Even as it was, the pinch for money to move the crops in the fall of 1887 was so severe that Cleveland thought for a time of calling an extra session. Common sense and common justice required a reduction in the volume of taxes. In his tariff message, Cleveland rejected the suggestion that internal revenue taxes be reduced—he thought the levies on liquor and tobacco socially proper. It was the tariff taxes that ought to be cut, he declared; taxes which fell on every farmer and workingman, injured every consumer of manufactured goods, and operated to restrict the foreign market for American foodstuffs and other materials, since Europe could buy only in proportion as it sold. The tariff message was really unanswerable. But it gave Cleveland's opponents an opportunity to appeal to a variety of selfish interests, and to make the tariff issue the central topic of a presidential campaign filled with misrepresentation and prejudice.

No subject was more frequently treated by cartoonists between the Civil War and First World War than the tariff, many of the arguments used being stock party slogans. To give it freshness and dramatic appeal required considerable ingenuity. Keppler's cartoon had genuine force.

THE GOOSE THAT LAYS THE GOLDEN EGGS
BY BERNHARD GILLAM
[1888]

THE TARIFF QUESTION was the central issue of the Cleveland-Harrison campaign of 1888—thrust into the open by Cleveland's uncompromising tariff message. In the East the Republicans filled the industrial areas with propaganda which linked high tariffs with high wages. Protectionist tracts and posters were scattered throughout mill towns. Petitions against lowering the tariff were sent around to factories and shops, and foremen were asked to obtain signatures. Wheels were stopped while employees were asked to declare against a ruinous "free trade." Republican speakers denied that the tariff had anything whatever to do with the trusts, and predicted depression, unemployment, and general misery if the Democrats put lower duties into effect. Harrison had the support of one of the most prominent labor leaders, Terence V. Powderly, the head of the Knights of Labor. This Republican cartoon, which shows Representative Roger Q. Mills, author of the pending Mills Bill for a reduction of the tariff, trying to seduce the honest workingman into slaying the goose Protection, appeared in Republican *Judge* for September 8, 1888.

A HYDRA THAT MUST BE CRUSHED AND THE SOONER THE BETTER
BY JOSEPH KEPPLER
[1888]

MEANWHILE THE DEMOCRATS emphasized the argument that the steep Civil War tariff still on the statute books was the hydra from which sprang the venomous heads of all the trusts—the coal trust, the lead trust, the steel trust, the oil trust, the sugar trust, and many more. The thesis could hardly be more graphic than Keppler made it in his cartoon, published in *Puck* on March 7, 1888. Is Uncle Sam going to be allowed to swing his club marked Law? Henry George made numerous speeches to Eastern workingmen attacking high protection, but he rather overshot the mark by asking for free trade. Cleveland, in his letter of acceptance, delivered himself of several epigrams. "Unnecessary taxation is unjust taxation," he asserted. He declared that the people asked relief from an undue burden of taxes—and the Republicans offered instead "free tobacco and free whiskey." But the battle went against the Democrats, and one reason was that most Eastern workingmen and Middle Western farmers swallowed the protectionist arguments.

BOSSES OF THE SENATE
BY JOSEPH KEPPLER
[1889]

WHEN THIS CARTOON APPEARED, the Senate seemed filling up with rich men representing great corporate interests. *Harper's Weekly* had remarked that the Senate was popularly regarded as "a club of rich men," and that some of these plutocrats did not hesitate to vote upon questions in which they had a pecuniary interest. It contained James G. Fair of Nevada, 1881–87, probably worth thirty millions; Leland Stanford, who hade made a huge fortune from the Central Pacific; John P. Jones of Nevada, who had grown enormously rich from silver mines; J. N. Camden, who had accumulated immense wealth in railroads, iron, coal, and petroleum; and numerous others of the same type. When in 1890 Calvin S. Brice, a man without recognized qualifications other than riches, was elected Senator from Ohio, the *Nation* declared that control of the government seemed to be passing into new hands. Once lawyers and journalists and soldiers of eminence had dominated it. "But their day began to pass when the great speculators, the oil, coal, iron, and railroad men, began to appear on the scene under the influence of the immense premiums offered to money-making talent by the debased currency, the high tariff, and the opening of the great West by the new lines of railroad. The talent of the country then began to be turned into the money-making field." It was natural that, rich men having become popular heroes, they should also get popular support for high political office. When they did not get the votes of the people, they could buy those of the State legislatures. Already reformers were urging popular election of Senators as a remedy for the corruption in the legislative choice of these officers.

But what alarmed careful observers far more than the appearance of rich men in high governmental posts was the fact that they more or less openly acted as servants of great corporations. Don Cameron of Pennsylvania was subservient to the Pennsylvania Railroad; Nelson W. Aldrich of Rhode Island to the powerful manufacturing companies of his State; Gorman of Maryland to the Central Maryland Railroad; Allison of Iowa to the railroads which crossed that State; Edward Murphy, who presently entered the Senate from New York, to the mills and factories of such centers as his own home, Troy; and various Western Senators to the big ranching and lumbering interests. Who, in such a body, would represent the common man? Keppler, in this picture of the trusts as human-headed money-bags, eloquently posed this question. The cartoon also represents the popular demand that was to bring about the enactment next year of the Sherman Anti-Trust Act, a law which at first proved quite ineffective.

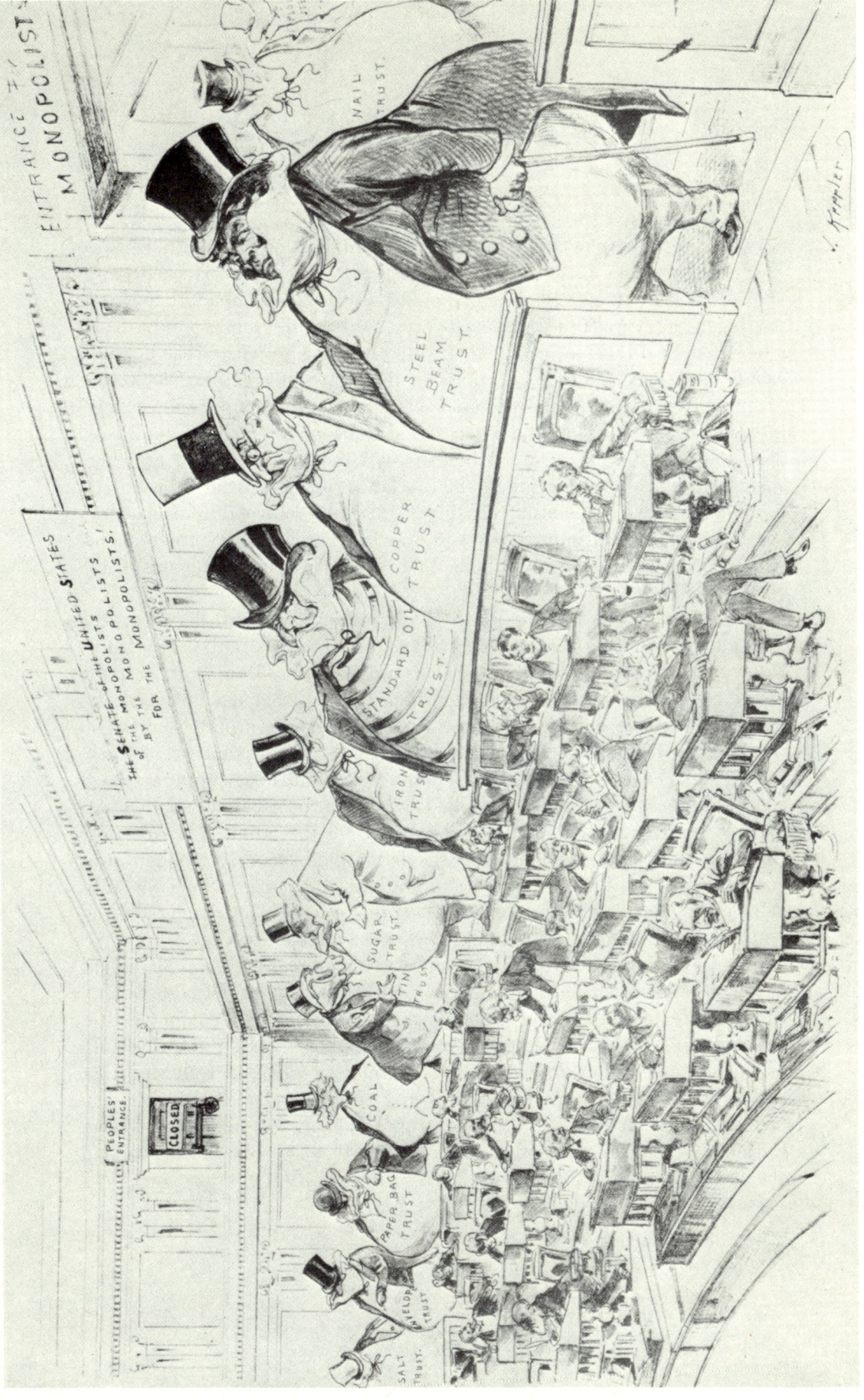

A COLD RECEPTION EVERYWHERE

BY JOSEPH KEPPLER

[1889]

PROHIBITION HAD BEEN an important issue in the United States ever since the original "Maine Law" was passed in the northeastern State in 1851. The tide swelled before the Civil War, then ebbed, then slowly swelled again. Always the cartoonists presented Prohibition as a dour, hard-jawed, fanatical Puritan; we have already seen that in "The Great Republican Reform Party of 1856." Keppler in his first comic paper, *Die Vehme* (September 18, 1869), had pictured a "member of a temperance society" in battered high hat, long-tailed coat, and tight trousers, with a bluish-red nose and an umbrella. In a cartoon in *Puck* in 1886 he used a grim, bespectacled harridan to personify the dry laws. Finally, in the amusing and forcible picture here given (*Puck*, July 3, 1889), he returned to his first conception, with a great improvement in drawing, amplifying it into a symbol which anticipated the figure whom Rollin Kirby later made famous in the New York *World*.

A cold shoulder is here given by three New England States on the right and four Southern States on the left side of the street, with Pennsylvania thrown in, to Mr. Prohibition and his water-bottle. But in other parts of the country he was doing better. Maine still had her dry law, and was making spasmodic efforts at enforcement. In Iowa the prohibitionists had won a great triumph in 1886, passing the Clark Act to shut up all those "moral sinks," the saloons. South Carolina was about to set up a system of county dispensaries, rigidly controlled by a State board. Local option was making progress in great parts of the West and the South. The Woman's Christian Temperance Union, under the determined Frances E. Willard, was energetically maintaining its crusade, and the still more formidable Anti-Saloon League, which operated on the principle of blackmailing the old parties into cooperation, was about to become a national power.

If Keppler had realized that a continuous fight was necessary, he might have followed up the idea here expressed. As it was, he left the field to Kirby, who imposed his conception on the imagination of the country after national prohibition became effective. When Arthur Bartlett Maurice published his brochure *How They Draw Prohibition* (1930), it showed that Kirby's figure, more gaunt, forbidding, and intolerant than that here given, (which has a trace of weak old-soak-ism), had greatly influenced Weed, Enright, Fitzpatrick, and other latter-day cartoonists. But the artists had always used a thin, glum, hatchet-faced man to typify the "crank."

ONE SLAVE AND MANY MASTERS

BY JOSEPH KEPPLER

[1889]

How fares the civil service?—such was almost the first question that reformers asked regarding the Harrison Administration. The answer had to be mixed. Harrison had succeeded to a Democrat; his party was hungry for offices. Within six months Assistant Postmaster-General Clarkson had made 20,000 changes in the post offices, while the President and Secretary Windom of the Treasury had been busy rooting Democrats out of the custom houses and internal revenue offices. This was not done to please themselves. It was to oblige the heads of the party machines in the various States—Foraker in Ohio, Platt in New York, Mahone in Virginia, Quay in Pennsylvania, Dudley in Indiana, and Clarkson himself in Iowa. The Irish voters and the Grand Army of the Republic had to be placated. Keppler hits off the situation aptly enough in his drawing of the spoils system treadmill. But it had another and better side. All the circumstances considered, Harrison's civil service record was fairly good. He made Theodore Roosevelt civil service commissioner, and it need not be said that Roosevelt was highly efficient. He enlarged the classified civil service list from 27,000 to 38,000 positions. This was the sort of cartoon that strengthened his hand against the bosses and did a public service by fastening attention on their whip-cracking tactics. From this time forward—so thoroughly was the merit system entrenching itself in public favor—the old spoils abuses, which had been constantly in the public eye since our cartoon of 1834 entitled "Office Hunters," ceased to attract much attention. When Harrison came up for renomination in 1892, both the party bosses and the most radical of the civil service reformers were against him; evidence that he had pursued a moderate path.

The cartoon appeared in *Puck* of September 18, 1889.

Puck, as appears in the text accompanying "No Welcome for the Little Stranger" in the present volume, fought valiantly for this cause.

"THE MINORITY BE D----D!"

BY LOUIS DALRYMPLE
[1890]

ONE OF THE MOST DRAMATIC moments of American parliamentary history occurred on January 29, 1890, when the newly elected Speaker, Thomas B. Reed, took charge of the House with dictatorial vigor. That House of Representatives, like several of its recent predecessors, was closely divided between Democrats and Republicans; and if the old rules had been left standing, it would have been practically impossible to transact any business on which the two parties did not agree. Particularly obstructive was a rule which permitted a member, though present and in his seat, to count himself "absent" simply by refusing to answer the roll-call. No business could be done without a majority of the House, for the Constitution requires a quorum, and nothing less than a majority was a quorum. If all the Democrats declined to answer the roll-call, and even a few Republicans were absent or disgruntled, the House would lack its quorum, and its work would come to a standstill. This had happened again and again in the past. But Reed was determined that it should happen no more. The Harrison Administration had just come into power; it was anxious to write on the statute books a number of important laws, including what became known as the McKinley Tariff. On the day named, therefore, Speaker Reed ordered the clerk to call the roll of the House, and to mark as present all those who were in their seats whether they answered the roll or not. A fierce storm of protest arose. Scores of Democrats leaped to their feet, denouncing the Speaker. But the clerk imperturbably droned on with the roll-call, and marked the protesting minority members present. With the Republican majority solidly behind him on the issue, Reed sustained his ruling—and indeed, later on the Democrats themselves adopted it. The Harrison Administration was thus placed in a position to pass the bills it wanted.

The burly Tom Reed, a giant more than six feet three in height and of 250 to 275 pounds in weight, with a bland and chubby face, lent himself well to caricature. He had a delightful wit, and many of his sayings—"A statesman is a successful politician who is dead," for example—will be long quoted. Dalrymple, in this cartoon published in *Puck* on February 5, 1890, indicts his "new arbitrary rules" harshly. But few men ever felt unkind toward the much caricatured Reed, and parliamentary experts and political historians have long agreed that his efficient rules had become an absolute necessity if Congress was to do its work. Under him and Cannon they became a little *too* efficient—that was all.

NONE BUT MILLIONAIRES NEED APPLY —THE COMING STYLE OF PRESIDENTIAL ELECTION

BY JOSEPH KEPPLER

[1890]

Not merely was the Senate filling up with millionaires; plutocracy seemed to be laying its grimy paw on the presidency. A candidate did not necessarily have to be rich in his own right, but he had to appeal to men of wealth who would loosen their money-bags. Nobody knew how much Matthew Quay (the Republican national chairman) and John Wanamaker spent in 1888 to put Benjamin Harrison in the White House, for Quay wisely burned his records immediately after the election; but the sum unquestionably broke all records. Special steps were taken to "fry the fat" out of rich manufacturers seeking high-tariff benefits. Moreover, in the critical States of New York and Indiana much of the money was used dishonestly. In Indiana it went to buy up the large purchasable vote—"divide the floaters into blocks of five," had been the injunction; in New York it went to sway certain local machine-groups in New York City. The men and corporations who made large campaign contributions expected favors in return, and got them. In 1896, even the relatively poor candidate Bryan had his rich backers in the silver-mine owners of the Mountain States, and mine-owners contributed to the Bryan fund in the hope of a huge return in enhanced silver prices. Keppler does not mean that Collis P. Huntington and Leland Stanford, Calvin S. Brice and Henry M. Flagler, could buy their way into the Presidency; he means that they and their like could gain a hold on the party managers who made the Presidents. W. W. Dudley, who holds up the Presidential chair, had been treasurer of the Republican campaign in 1888, and author of the blocks-of-five circular. In the foreground it is interesting to note the coarse face of Abel Rathbone Corbin, the stock-market operator who had got close to Grant by marrying his sister, and had played a key part in the Black Friday affair. It is also interesting to note President Sidney Dillon of the Union Pacific, who had been connected with the Credit Mobilier. Russell Sage, it will be seen, is making a very frugal bid, while Jay Gould seems disinclined to part with any money whatever. The influence of money in politics was dealt with in various other cartoons, for example Keppler's "Triumph of Boodle" (April 17, 1889—the people's vote enslaved by "Monopoly" and "Bribery"), "Bosses of the Senate" (1890—reproduced in the present volume), and "Bidding for his Vote" (1888—politicians seeking the Grand Army vote).

THE NATIONAL GRAB-BAG—
"HELP YOURSELF"

BY JOSEPH KEPPLER

[1890]

THE HARRISON ADMINISTRATION had its own method of dealing with the plethora of Federal funds which it found on taking office in 1889. "God help the surplus!" said "Corporal" James Tanner, who had a brief career as Commissioner of Pensions, and whose principle was to make a grant to "every old comrade that needs it." A Dependent Pension Bill was passed, giving every veteran a pension of at least six dollars a month if dependent—whether his service had been good or bad, and whether his disability had its origin in the war or in delirium tremens. Extravagant appropriations were made for public buildings. The direct tax collected from the States during the Civil War was refunded to them. Rivers and harbors were improved at great expense; President Chester A. Arthur had vetoed an internal improvement bill of wasteful character, but Harrison made no objection to more lavish grants. The Administration was more responsive to special interests, in fact, than any since Grant's. Harrison had been elected on a platform which made a variety of promises to pressure groups—to the Western silver men, to manufacturers demanding high protection, to the G.A.R. asking pensions, and so on. It had to make good these rash promises. The result was the Sherman Silver Purchase Act, which provided for Federal purchase of four and a half million ounces of silver bullion every month, or almost the entire output of the American mines; the McKinley Tariff, which raised custom duties to the highest level thus far reached; laws and rulings which raised the pensions expenditure from $98,000,000 when Harrison entered office to $157,000,000 the year he left it; and other enactments here illustrated. The surplus disappeared, and the gold reserve in the Treasury sank to a dangerously low level. As it did so, the economic and financial skies all over the world turned black—the first grave portent of the stormy times being the suspension of the great house of Baring in London in 1890.

Keppler illustrates his conception of President Harrison's littleness not only by placing him under his grandfather's big beaver, but by contrasting him with the bulky Tom Reed, and the tall J. J. Ingalls, Senator from Kansas —both of whom warmly approved of legislation for special interests. The cartoon appeared in *Puck* for April 16, 1890, as the Republicans were beginning a busy legislative season.

THE RAVEN

BY JOSEPH KEPPLER

[1890]

"QUOTH THE RAVEN, nevermore!" Little Benjamin Harrison, almost lost under the big hat of his grandfather William Henry Harrison, is appalled as at midnight Raven-Blaine perches on the bust of the old Indian fighter and utters the fateful word. The cartoon was inspired by the obvious disagreement between President Harrison and Secretary of State Blaine over the McKinley Tariff, which was pending when the drawing appeared in *Puck* of August 13, 1890. Harrison stood for high and undiluted protection. Blaine stood instead for concessions which would permit reciprocity with the nations of Latin America—and in particular for a reduction in the proposed duties upon sugar. "There is not a section or a line in the entire [McKinley] bill," he wrote in July, "that will open a market for another bushel of wheat or another barrel of pork." These were harsh words, for the Republican leaders had been trying hard to persuade the farmers that the McKinley Tariff would benefit them. But back of the disagreement of Blaine and Harrison over reciprocity there lay deeper, more important, differences. They differed on foreign relations, Harrison wishing to take a stiffer stand on various questions than Blaine found politic. Their wives disliked one another, for Mrs. Blaine could never forget that she might well have been mistress of the White House. And the two leaders were temperamentally antipathetic, for Blaine was quick, sympathetic, emotional, and active, while Harrison was cautious, unimaginative, self-centered, and frigid. By 1890 Blaine and the other principal party chieftains had decided that Harrison would have only one term. On the eve of the Republican Convention in 1892 Blaine dramatically resigned from the Cabinet—thus advertising the fact that he had no use for the President, and hoped to see him denied a renomination.

This cartoon, in *Puck* of August 13, 1890, was spread over two pages, with only two figures. In the wide space between the diminutive Harrison and the sinister, croaking Blaine there is a play of light and shade which is seldom encountered in political cartoons, and which reflects Keppler's artistic aspirations. Indeed, this bit of chiaroscuro greatly heightens the effect of a highly dramatic piece of work. The cartoon belonged to a series in which Keppler dealt with the two men. In *Puck* of July 18, 1888, for example, he showed Harrison as a cigar-store wooden Indian, taking the place of Blaine in similar guise, relegated to the ash-barrel. On March 6, 1889, he presented Harrison as Little Lord Fauntleroy standing beside the huge grim watchdog Blaine. Finally, on October 7, 1891, in "Victims of Temporary Aberration," Blaine, Harrison and McKinley are grouped together as claiming all credit for prosperity.

WILL IT RISE?

BY F. VICTOR GILLAM

[1896]

GROVER CLEVELAND in his second Administration, 1893–97, waged a desperate, heroic, and successful struggle to maintain the currency on a gold basis; that is, to keep silver money and paper money at parity with gold money. At times it seemed likely that he would lose the battle. Only four successive sales of government bonds sufficed to keep an adequate gold reserve in the Treasury. The most dangerous moment was at the end of January, 1895, when for several days the stock of gold at the Sub-Treasury in New York was almost exhausted, and men feared that the country would be forced to a silver basis. This would have dislocated our financial relations with the gold-standard nations of Europe, and given another severe shock to credit and business confidence; it would doubtless have been highly disastrous. The depression following the panic of 1893 was terrible enough anyway. In 1895 J. P. Morgan and August Belmont came to the rescue of the government, forming a syndicate which brought gold from Europe. But the bankers were popularly believed to have driven a very hard bargain. When in January, 1896, it became necessary to sell the fourth issue of bonds, it was therefore offered for public subscription. Men waited anxiously to learn whether it would carry the Treasury to safety—and it did. Stocks of gold rose, and no further sales were required. Altogether, Cleveland sold $293,-000,000 worth of bonds; but he saved the country from going to a fifty- or sixty-cent dollar as measured in gold, and shortened the depression.

The Republicans of course made capital out of the embarrassments of the President. This cartoon by the brother of Bernhard Gillam, in *Judge* for March 7, 1896, is thoroughly hostile. Cleveland, by burning bonds, has gotten the gold reserve up between fifty and sixty millions, little more than halfway to the goal of one hundred millions. His halo has fallen from his head. The icy storm sweeping the country is labeled "Free Trade Deficit." This was of course quite unfair. The Treasury deficit had been caused by Republican extravagance under Harrison, and by the steep McKinley Tariff, which was so prohibitive that in large trade areas it completely cut off revenue. When Cleveland took office the Treasury reserve had sunk so low that the Republican Administration had prepared plates for a bond issue. The panic of 1893 was not a Democratic panic, nor did it have any connection with the Wilson Tariff passed by the Democrats, which did not become law until late in 1894. But a president is usually blamed for everything that goes wrong during his term of office.

POLITICAL PIRATES

BY CHARLES J. TAYLOR

[1896]

THE FREE-SILVER MEN who have seized the Democratic ship, hoisting the sail "Popocracy," have disguised themselves and are trying to get near enough to the full-laden vessel "National Prosperity" to board and loot her. Here are good portraits of all the principal "Popocrats": Altgeld of Illinois, Tillman of South Carolina, Peffer of Kansas, Blackburn of Kentucky, Sulzer and David B. Hill of New York, and the rich mine owner W. M. Stewart of Nevada. As decoys they are using the Prohibitionist John P. St. John, the Maine capitalist and shipbuilder Arthur Sewall (nominee this year for Vice President), and the famous female orator Mary Ellen Lease. Bryan is playing his best siren air. The cartoon is an adaptation from a once well known painting by the French artist François Auguste Biard, which became popular after its exhibition in London in 1855. At least twice before it supplied the theme of an American cartoon. In *Vanity Fair* in the sixties, American publishers appear as pirates of literary property; and in *Harper's Weekly*, November 9, 1872, " 'The Pirates' under False Colors" are Greeley and his followers. But it specially lent itself to this attack on the free-silver men. Many conservatives in 1896 would have regarded the word "pirate" as not a whit too strong for Altgeld (often miscalled an anarchist), Peffer and Tillman. It remained for a later generation to do justice to the honesty, patriotism, and abounding courage of these men, and to the fine qualities of Bryan himself. But in those days Populism and free silver were attacked and ridiculed in many a cartoon. It is worth noting that Democratic *Puck* (in which this cartoon appeared on September 23, 1896) and Republican *Judge* this year united in attacking Bryan and his associates.

Of Bryan cartoons enough exist to fill a good-sized volume. Among those of merit which appeared in the next few years were J. S. Pughe's "Busted" (*Puck*, December 20, 1899), which depicts Bryan, Pulitzer, E. L. Godkin and others as shabby actors walking the rails; Louis Dalrymple's "A Hint Not Taken" (*Puck*, September 26, 1900), in which Labor repudiates Bryan and sixteen-to-one; and Victor Gillam's "Don Quixote Bryan Meets Disaster" (*Judge*, November 10, 1900—reproduced in the present volume), presenting Bryan as overthrown by the flailing arms of a windmill labelled "Full Dinner Pail." And well into the twentieth century we find the younger Keppler (*Puck*, September 25, 1907) picturing Bryan as a "Democratic Micawber" waiting for something to turn up, and S. Ehrhart (*Puck*, July 3, 1907) imagining a "Democratic Eden," with Adam Bryan much disliking the serpent Hearst.

A MAN OF MARK
BY HOMER DAVENPORT
[1896]

FRIGHTENED LITTLE McKinley, under the thumb of Mark Hanna, is powerfully descriptive of the situation as the cartoonist saw it. Hearst's New York *Journal*, one of the few important Eastern papers supporting Bryan, published this cartoon to offset the still harsher and more scurrilous depictions of Bryan in the conservative press. A number of politicians, editors, and caricaturists tried to create the legend that McKinley was a nonentity raised to power by the wily Cleveland capitalist Hanna. There was no truth in this malignant fiction. McKinley had been a gallant Civil War officer; by laborious study he made himself an expert on the tariff question; he gave his name to the most famous tariff bill of the latter half of the century. He had a capacity for growth. In the intercourse between McKinley and Hanna the former nearly always led. But in a certain large sense the cartoon has some truth. McKinley was to a greater extent than he realized the creature and agent of those great forces which Mark Hanna typified.

THE TANTALUS OF TO-DAY
BY J. S. PUGHE
[1897]

THE CREED of the Gold Democrats or Cleveland Democrats, and of a large number of liberal Republicans, is well set forth in this *Puck* cartoon: the creed of John G. Carlisle, Richard Olney, William C. Whitney, Abram S. Hewitt, Carl Schurz, Charles W. Eliot, George Haven Putnam, and many more. A lower tariff, a stable currency—these they regarded as the chief requisites for attaining general prosperity, more justly distributed. Half of their demands were about to be met. The silverites, decisively defeated in 1896, were loosening their end of the rope. A pronounced increase in world production of gold, attributable mainly to increased output in South Africa and discoveries in the Klondike, was about to provide a needed expansion of the currency. But the tariff rope was bound tighter than ever this year by the Dingley Bill.

Puck lived on with slowly diminishing luster until 1918. New conditions in journalism, not deficiency in talent, furnished the explanation of its decline. It had made a fine fight for many good causes, and this cartoon shows that it was still fighting.

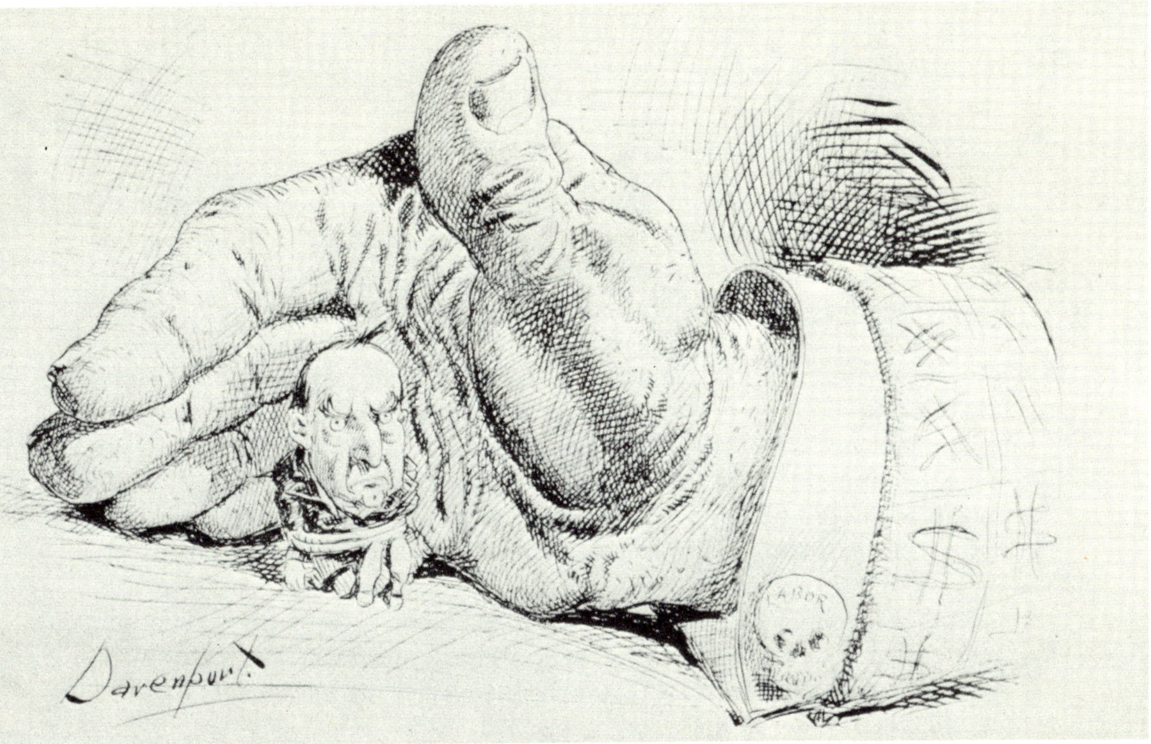

SHE IS GETTING TOO FEEBLE TO HOLD THEM
BY J. S. PUGHE
[1896]

REBELLION broke out in Cuba in 1895; it held the horrified attention of Americans. Misgovernment by Spain was flagrant. A corrupt bureaucracy of Spanish placeholders dominated the general government and the municipalities, using their position to enrich themselves. Taxation was atrociously high, yet the insular debt constantly grew. Mercantilist restrictions compelled Cubans to buy many necessities from Spanish manufacturers at exorbitant prices. Arbitrary arrests and summary executions were frequent; the courts were often mere agencies for extortion. Education was so badly supported that the mass of the population was illiterate. The impoverished island was badly off at all times; when in 1894 the Wilson Tariff put an end to a reciprocity arrangement which had benefited Cuban sugar growers, the depression was accentuated. As for the Philippines, José Rizal and other leaders had long conducted a campaign against the corrupt and selfish friars, who had control of wide estates, and against administrative tyranny. It seemed clear that the Spanish government was incapable of discharging its responsibilities.

TIME NEARLY UP
BY JOSEPH KEPPLER, JR.
[1897]

THE SAVAGE COURSE of the war in Cuba gradually made it seem nearly intolerable to Americans. Spain's large armies were resisted by the population under tested leaders—Maximo Gomez, José Marti, Calixto Garcia, and others. No quarter was given on either side. The policy of the insurgents was to lay waste all parts of the island that might be used by the Spaniards; the devastation became frightful. When the Spaniards herded hundreds of thousands of noncombatants, chiefly women, children, and old men, into concentration camps, with insufficient food and no sanitary arrangements, great suffering and loss of life ensued. The war cost Americans, who had investments of fifty millions in the island and an annual trade of a hundred millions with it, considerable sums. But it was the general inhumanity that chiefly angered Americans. A time came in 1897 when it was generally agreed that if Spain did not soon make arrangements for peace, the United States would have to intervene. Here Uncle Sam says: "It's a good rule, when you're mad, to count twenty before you speak; but, by Jingo! I'm up to seventeen, now!"

THE CARES OF A GROWING FAMILY
BY J. CAMPBELL CORY
[1898]

THE MOMENT Dewey struck at Manila, it was plain that the United States was likely to have a family of dependencies. Did it want them? Many said yes, and talked about Duty and Destiny. Others declared that the European virus of imperialistic subjugation and exploitation must never get into our veins, that the government had been erected for the welfare of the American people alone, and if it undertook to carry benefits to every misgoverned island with which it came into contact, it would be in trouble all over the globe. Imperialism would have a bad effect on the national character. If, after taking Hawaii, we also took the Philippines, Schurz prophesied that our land-lust would be hard to satisfy. Most Americans refused to take such dark predictions seriously. McKinley waited for public sentiment to crystallize on the question of annexing the Philippines. Then the Administration accepted the general trend toward acquisition of nearly all Spanish colonies excepting Cuba.

The issue went into the campaign of 1900. If we kept the Philippines and Puerto Rico, Bryan argued, we would need a large army and navy to protect them, and would steadily develop appetite for imperial power.

"YES, WILLIE, NURSE HAS HAD TO SIT ON TEDDY"
BY FREDERICK B. OPPER
[1900]

OPPER GAVE the Hearst newspapers a series of cartoons on the McKinley Administration supposedly dominated by Hanna and the trusts; cartoons with an outward aspect of harmless drollery, but at bottom bitter enough, and inculcating the idea that the common man was remorselessly oppressed by special interests. The Hearst press, strongly Democratic, anti-British and anti-plutocratic, insisted that Hanna, wedded to big business, was the real arbiter of affairs in Washington; McKinley was good-naturedly obedient, and Roosevelt an exhibitionist who had never grown up. In 1900 Hanna was very unwillingly converted to the nomination of Roosevelt for the vice presidency; he thought him too obstreperous.

At this time caricature was becoming more journalistic. As the daily newspaper took over this line of endeavor and the comic weeklies began to disappear, the cartoonist often gave less attention to careful draughtsmanship, and furnished reporting rather than interpretation, and raillery rather than satire.

THE WHITTLER FOR THE WORLD
BY F. VICTOR GILLAM
[1899]

By the end of the century the United States was an industrial giant, and had embarked upon a career of economic imperialism. Its huge business units were marketing American goods all over the globe. The Standard Oil had worsted the Russian petroleum interests in the battle for the rich European market, and sold its wares literally from China to Peru. The Carnegie steel mills for a time in the late nineties undersold British manufacturers of rails in the English market. From the wheatfields of Hungary and Russia, Argentina and Australia, rose the clatter of the reapers sold by the International Harvester Company. The Duke interests scattered American tobacco over the world; the Singer and other companies had made American sewing machines familiar everywhere; American typewriters, cash registers, fountain pens, and telephones were common in most business offices. The year in which this cartoon was published saw the United States produce nearly five billion dollars' worth of agricultural products, and nearly eleven and a half billion dollars' worth of manufactured goods. These figures were small compared with those which the country would attain in the next twenty years, but they were large enough to give Americans a sense of pride. Great Britain had long been the workshop of the world; now the palm was passing to the United States, and it would remain there. Prosperity had come back with rapid pace during the years 1897–99, brought in by the revival of business confidence following McKinley's election, by the flow of new streams of gold from the Klondike and South Africa, by the war contracts of the Spanish conflict and the flush of success that followed victory, and by favorable crop-marketing conditions abroad. Americans looked forward to a splendid future in selling foodstuffs and manufactured goods to Europe, to the fast-developing nations of Latin America, and to teeming Asia. Victor Gillam's exuberant cartoon in *Judge*, July 1, 1899, is typical of much comment of the time.

The growing international trade seemed to many to herald a breakdown of the oldtime American isolation, and President McKinley agreed. When he spoke at Buffalo just before his assassination, he said that the encouragement of foreign commerce must be one of the great concerns of the country. "The period of exclusiveness is past. The expansion of our trade and commerce is the pressing problem. Commercial wars are unprofitable. A policy of good will and friendly trade relations will prevent reprisals."

DON QUIXOTE BRYAN MEETS DISASTER IN HIS FIGHT AGAINST JUDGE'S "FULL DINNER-PAIL"

BY F. VICTOR GILLAM

[1900]

THE CAMPAIGN OF 1900 was a very different story from that of 1896. Once more Bryan and McKinley were the opposing candidates; once more Hanna was the Republican campaign manager. But in what Bryan called "the first battle" the contest was close to the very end, and the Republicans had to raise money frantically and spend it prodigally. In the "second battle" the odds were overwhelmingly against Bryan from the beginning. McKinley, always a lovable man, now stood at the apex of his popularity. He could point to an Administration which had been in most respects markedly successful. The promised legislation had been enacted. The long-impending war with Spain had been won without a single reverse. Whereas in 1896 the farmers had been arrayed against the businessmen, and the South and West against the North and East, now harmony filled the nation. But above all, prosperity had come back. Factories were running at full blast, employment at good wages was abundant, and agricultural prices had improved. To be sure, what was later called "big business" was in control. McKinley's Cabinet had been dominated by wealthy men of corporation connections, while the Senate was notoriously managed in the interests of large business units by Hanna, Nelson A. Aldrich, Orville Platt, William B. Allison, and a few others. But the existence of the "full dinner-pail," long a Republican slogan, was incontestable. There it stood. Its supports, according to the Republican platform, were the gold standard, the protective tariff, and protection of workers from contract immigration and convict labor. When Don Quixote Bryan hurled himself against the pail, he was quickly unhorsed. McKinley won by an electoral vote of 292 to 155, with a plurality of 860,000 in a total vote of about 13,700,000. He and his party were justified in declaring that the voters had endorsed the policy of territorial expansion.

Other anti-Bryan cartoons of this period are noted in connection with the cartoon "Political Pirates" (1896) in the present volume. And the caricaturists kept up the fight against Bryan well into the twentieth century.

TWENTY YEARS AFTER

BY J. S. PUGHE

[1902]

THE JEST ABOUT one party catching another in swimming and stealing its clothes dates back to Disraeli's introduction of a new Parliamentary Reform Bill in 1856. He wished to see the Conservative Party stay in power, and stole Gladstone's measures in order to ingratiate himself with the British workingmen. More than once American politicians have purloined each other's wares. Even Jefferson stole a great deal of old Federalist thunder, strengthening the national government while he protested that it must be kept weak. But it is the third parties whose doctrines have been most ruthlessly filched—once the public has been converted to their soundness. In the early nineties the Populist tenets were denounced as exhibitions of sheer lunacy and wild ebullitions of class prejudice. A generation later they had virtually all been placed on the statute books. The Republicans under Theodore Roosevelt and then the Democrats under Woodrow Wilson wrote one Populist demand after another into law.

Pughe's cartoon shows a realization that a new era had dawned in American history. Theodore Roosevelt had taken control of the Republican Party and the government in 1901; already it was plain that the G.O.P. was seizing upon new policies. They were the very policies that the Democrats—or rather the Populists *and* Democrats—had lately espoused. Roosevelt in his message to Congress in December, 1901, had outlined most of the reform measures that he was to put into effect in the ensuing seven years. He was eager to use his big stick on malefactors of great wealth, to promote the square deal for everybody, to befriend the farmer and workingman, and to conserve the national resources. Another year and the Bureau of Corporations would come into existence to apply "pitiless publicity" to monopolies, while the Elkins Act would abolish railroad rebates. McKinley himself, in his last speech, had indicated a belief that the Republican Party should adopt a more liberal policy on the tariff; a belief that Roosevelt rather mildly shared. Twenty years earlier, in 1882, Keppler had pictured the tattered Democratic Party seizing upon the garments that the Republicans ought to have worn, but had cast off to bathe in "corruption water"—tax reduction, civil service reform, lower tariffs, an isthmian canal. Now, and more aptly, Pughe showed the Republican Party renovating its habiliments; trust legislation, tariff reform, anti-monopoly, were a few of its new creeds. They had popular appeal, a fact which the Bryanite Democrats had forgotten in making free silver and anti-imperialism their chief planks. Roosevelt, fighting spectacular battles, was to make reform more soundly effective than any leader since Lincoln, and to win a great popular following as statesman and patriot.